The Sermon on the Mount

The Sermon on the Mount

A Personal Encounter with the Wisdom of Jesus

JAMES L. MAYFIELD

WIPF & STOCK · Eugene, Oregon

THE SERMON ON THE MOUNT
A Personal Encounter with the Wisdom of Jesus

Scripture quotations are from the Revised Standard Version of the Bible, copyright © 1946, 1952, and 1971 by the National Council of Churches of Christ in the United States.

Wipf & Stock
An Imprint of Wipf and Stock Publishers
199 W. 8th Ave., Suite 3
Eugene, OR 97401

www.wipfandstock.com

ISBN 13: 978-1-61097-696-1

Manufactured in the U.S.A.

To Rita

In love for who she is

And in gratitude for more than I can say

Contents

Preface

THIS BOOK IS THE culmination of personal experience and study during many years as pastor, teacher, and writer. On my various journeys through chapters 5–7 of the Gospel of Matthew, I have been assisted by the writings of recent biblical scholars, but most of all by six pastor-scholars from across the centuries: John Chrysostom, Augustine of Hippo, Martin Luther, John Calvin, John Wesley, and Dietrich Bonhoeffer.

I have tried to understand chapters 5–7 from the Gospel of Matthew within the context of the New Testament as a whole. When I have been confronted by a passage that is especially puzzling, I have tried to view it from the perspective of the New Testament as a whole and strived to understand it in the light of other passages of the Bible that are more clear and obviously consistent with the bulk of the New Testament writings

REGARDING THE FORMAT OF THE BOOK

The reader will notice that I have not chosen to begin each chapter quoting the passage to be discussed. I have chosen to make comments about the passage first and then quote the passage at the end of the chapter. My intention is to provide introductory material that will awaken sensitivities so that at the end of each chapter, when the passage from Matthew is read, it will come alive with meaning. Also, at the end of each chapter are questions that are intended to be helpful in meditation and conversation. My goal is to help the reader focus on the passage and comtemplate its meaning so that he or she experiences a personal encounter with the wisdom of Jesus.

WAYS TO USE THIS BOOK

This book can be read as any book is read. However, because the sayings of Jesus in the Sermon on the Mount are so rich, I recommend reading it at a deliberately slower pace—thinking and praying about each of these sayings of Jesus that Matthew quoted.

This book contains forty chapters plus a postscript. Why forty chapters? The reader probably remembers that Jesus spent forty days in prayer and meditation preparing for his ministry (Matt 4:2; Mark 1:13; Luke 4:1–2). My hope is that each day for forty days the reader will read one chapter and after reading that chapter will ponder the personal meaning and relevance of the passage from Matthew.

The wisdom to be found in these sayings of Jesus is appropriate for any time of the year and throughout the years of one's life; however, because in this book the Sermon on the Mount is discussed in forty chapters (plus a personal postscript), this book is ideally suited for the season of Lent. Of course, it is not intended to be limited to that time of the year. (See the reading schedules and the agenda for group conversations in the Appendix.)

The chapters related to the Beatitudes can stand alone and be used by themselves for personal meditation or for group conversation. The same is true for the verses related to prayer and the Lord's Prayer.

Acknowledgments

I AM GRATEFUL TO all the laity who were engaged in conversation with me regarding these passages—especially the men of Tarrytown United Methodist Church in Austin, Texas, who participated in the Wednesday Morning Bible Conversation, the participants in the Pastor's Bible Study Class 1988–90, and those members who participated in the first set of conversations dealing with earlier drafts of this book in 2008 and 2010.

I am grateful to Jim Hornfischer for encouraging me to write the book and his helpful suggestions regarding the first few drafts. I also am grateful to Carol Hall, who graciously read the manuscript with great care and gave me valuable help in making revisions and corrections. I am in debt to both of them for the hours they invested. Any errors that remain are mine, not theirs.

Most of all I am grateful to my wife, Rita, who in loving me through the many years of our marriage has been an instrument of God's amazing grace. In our dealing with good times and bad, she has taught me more about living the life of faith than all the books I have read or sermons and lectures I have heard.

1

Preparing for the Journey

PURPOSE OF THIS BOOK

THE PURPOSE OF THIS book is to help the reader *experience a personal encounter* with the wisdom of Jesus found in Matthew 5–7. As I wrote this book, the question I asked was, "What is the wisdom of Jesus in this passage, and what are the implications of that wisdom for daily living?"

THE SERMON ON THE MOUNT ACROSS THE CENTURIES

Across the centuries, as people thoughtfully and prayerfully read the Sermon on the Mount, many found more than intellectual theological wisdom. They found themselves encountered by the grace of God and not only enabled to face what they had to face but also empowered to move on. Through their wrestling with these sayings of Jesus, they were aided in discerning God's will as they dealt with the challenges they faced.

For example, in the century in which Christianity moved from being an outlawed religion to being the official religion of Rome, the Sermon on the Mount gave guidance to both John Chrysostom (347–407), who served as bishop in Constantinople, and Augustine (354–430), who served as bishop in Hippo, located in North Africa. During Augustine's lifetime, the western part of the Roman empire was being overrun by barbarians, and civilization as it had been known was thrown in turmoil. In the eastern part of the Mediterranean world, Chrysostom was faced with similar problems and crises. The church in the eastern and western parts of the Roman Empire was also in conflict regarding what gives life meaning (doctrine) and how to live (ethics). As both Chrysostom and Augustine dealt with the challenges they faced, they sought God's guidance and wisdom in the Sermon on the Mount.

In the social and religious upheaval known as the Reformation, both Martin Luther (1483–1546) and John Calvin (1509–1564) wrestled with problems of living in a situation in which the old order had collapsed and in which both church and state struggled against chaos. There were a variety of voices and powers trying to shape the emerging society. In the midst of the crises each of these men faced, they searched the Scriptures, including the Sermon on the Mount, to discern God's guidance for themselves and for the people who looked to them for leadership.

When the life and ministry of John Wesley (1703–1791) are discussed, it is not unusual for someone to declare that his work among the poor in eighteenth-century England was a significant factor in saving England from the kind of destructive revolution France experienced. The Sermon on the Mount was so important to Wesley that it was dealt with at length in thirteen of his forty-four sermons that served as a primary guide for Methodist leaders in the last half of the 1700s. These sermons continue to be part of the official "standards of doctrine" for the United Methodist Church, and are influential teachings for approximately seventy-five million Christians[1] around the world who are related to churches that trace their heritage through Wesley.

Dietrich Bonhoeffer (1906–1945) was a young German theologian and pastor whose ministry began about the time Adolph Hitler came to power, and it ended when Hitler had him hanged a few days before Germany surrendered. As Bonhoeffer struggled with what is required to be a faithful Christian in the midst of Nazi Germany, he wrote *The Cost of Discipleship*. More than one hundred pages are devoted to Bonhoeffer's attempt to discern the meaning in these sayings of Jesus for all people but especially for those struggling to live under tyranny.

MY EXPERIENCE WITH THESE SAYINGS OF JESUS

Throughout my forty-five years as a pastor, I have returned again and again to this mountain of proclamations, with first one guide and then

---

1. This statistic is taken from a 2011 public letter by George H. Freeman, General Secretary of the World Methodist Council.

another. The reason I have continued to return to these sayings of Jesus is that they are timeless, and therefore as relevant for our lives as when they were first spoken, or in the days of Chrysostom, Augustine, Luther, Calvin, Wesley or Bonhoeffer.

Today, even though I am familiar with this territory, I continue to discover new insights behind "this phrase" and under "that word"—wisdom I failed to notice on previous visits. Often what causes me to see a familiar passage anew is the way the sunlight and shadows of my experiences play upon these ancient rocks of truth.

MORE THAN INSIGHTS AND IDEAS

For persons of faith, the Sermon on the Mount is much more than a classic collection of profoundly wise sayings attributed to Jesus. For those who call themselves Christians, these sayings are part of Holy Scripture, what Christians sometimes call "the living Word of God."

To be sure, among Christians there are a wide variety of opinions about what it means to call the Bible and passages such as the Sermon on the Mount "the Word of God." It is also obvious to the most casual observer that Christians disagree with one another regarding how to read and interpret the Bible, including passages such as Matthew 5–7.

Nevertheless, Christians do agree that when people humbly and honestly open themselves with all their fears, hopes, pain, and joy to the Bible, and do this consistently and prayerfully over time, they gain more than knowledge, ideas, and insights. In time, they are encountered by the Holy Reality we call God, the One who is most clearly revealed in and through Jesus.

But for this encounter to happen, one must be open to the possibility of it happening. Reading Scripture is like participating in a significant conversation. If we approach a conversation convinced we already know what the other person is going to say, we will hear only what we were expecting to hear. But when we are open, when we give ourselves to the task of trying to discern what the other person really means (and do not get hung up on the way the message is being delivered), then genuine communication begins to happen.

In open and honest conversation, we do not always hear what we want to hear. So it is in our reading passages such as the Sermon on the Mount. There are times when we encounter soothing, healing, joyous truth that makes us profoundly happy (sometimes so happy we cry), but there are other times when what we discern Jesus saying is not what we want to hear, and our response is discomfort, even defensiveness or anger.

If, however, we hang on and wrestle with the truth, our experience has the potential of being like Jacob's wrestling through the darkness of the night (Gen 32:22–32). If we do not cut and run, sooner or later we discover that we, like Jacob, really are Israel (those who wrestle with God), and as was true of Jacob, who was given the new identity of Israel, we are no longer able to move through life in the way we did before this encounter. Our lives are changed, and changed for the better. This is a real possibility each time we open the Sermon on the Mount and open ourselves to the truth it reveals.

Across the centuries, faithful women and men have discovered that the Sermon on the Mount is like a classic work of art in that there is more to it than can be consumed in one encounter. Each time it is encountered there is the possibility of new discovery.

RELEVANT FOR TODAY

The wisdom of Jesus contained in the Sermon on the Mount is relevant for today. It is not merely wisdom for the people of Jesus' day. The issues he addressed are also issues of the twenty-first century. For example, the desire to experience faith and hope so that one can face whatever happens with a sense of purpose, peace, and hope is a desire that belongs to the present as much as to the past. Dealing with anger is a contemporary as well as an ancient challenge. In dealing with injustices, the temptation to give in to resentment, bitterness, and cynicism is as real today as in Jesus' day. The tendency toward hypocrisy that is rooted in the desire to be seen by others as a person of worth is as much a problem today as in New Testament times. Just as in the past, today it is easy in the midst of good times to drift into self-satisfaction, arrogantly looking down on those who are unable to do what we are doing or have what we have. Living through painful times, tragedies, and failures without giving in to self-pity, bitterness, or despair is as much a struggle today as in any period of history. Longing to live trusting God and God's love is not merely a longing of long ago.

The teachings of Jesus found in the Sermon on the Mount are not the sales pitch of some TV preacher promising a surefire way to health, wealth, and fun-filled happiness. These sayings do not advocate stoic endurance or optimistic, positive thinking as the means of shaping our daily living.

In the Sermon on the Mount, Jesus described through rather tough and realistic sayings what is involved in living what he called a blessed life regardless of whether the times are good or bad. This blessed life is a God-centered, ethical way of living that goes beyond superficial honesty, avoiding killing, stealing or other obvious acts of immorality. In these passages, Jesus speaks of justice beyond revenge and teaches those who will listen how to deal with their enemies. His wisdom points the way to inner peace that is not destroyed by the storms of life. Behind and beneath all these teachings is the generous mercy of God offering forgiveness for failure—forgiveness that Jesus teaches we are to offer to others. The way of living described in his teaching is daily living centered in God and committed to the good that is consistent with God's will.

For Meditation and Conversation

1. What do I hope to gain from spending forty days with these sayings of Jesus?

2. What issues, questions, or concerns do I bring with me to this experience?

2

The Way Jesus Teaches

MATTHEW 5:1–2

THE WAY MATTHEW TELLS the story, Jesus was in the hill country surrounding a large clear-water lake we call the Sea of Galilee. His ministry was off to a good start. As was true of anyone recognized as a man of God in those days, Jesus' ability to heal was seen by the public as verification that he really was a holy man worth listening to. The people knew (perhaps in a more literal way then than now) that a holy man or woman who could not offer some sort of healing was a waste of their time.

The more Jesus relieved the pains of living, the more people flocked to him. The passage known as the Sermon on the Mount begins with Jesus seeing a crowd coming toward him. He knew all these people were coming with deep longings, seeking hope for all their despairs, healing for all their hurts, rescue from all their problems, satisfaction for all their hungers. In short, people were coming to him with concerns only mildly different from concerns many of us have today.

Matthew tells us that when Jesus saw the crowd coming, he led his disciples to higher ground, both figuratively and literally. There Jesus began to teach his disciples.

With so many people gathering, why did he focus on his disciples rather than on the crowd? Why not turn this occasion into a massive healing service? My hunch is Jesus knew that the problems, pains, fears, and hopes the people brought to him were, in a sense, endless. He knew the burdens they brought were not limited to this multitude or to those who would be coming to him during his earthly ministry. I suspect Jesus knew more healing and hope were needed on earth than even the Son of God could distribute in one lifetime—especially a physical lifetime that was to be as brief as his and confined to such a tiny area on this planet. Those who followed him would have to carry on. His job was to train his followers, his students, his disciples. His job was to equip them. So, he climbed to higher ground and took the traditional position of a rabbi preparing to teach—he sat down.

On the surface, it seems his primary audience was the disciples who had left jobs and families in order to follow him. However, I am confident that Jesus was aware that he was not just teaching them. He was indirectly teaching at least three groups other than his disciples.

One of these groups was the women and men who followed Jesus wanting to learn more about what Jesus had to say and what it would be like to live the kind of life he proclaimed. They were followers of Jesus, the almost (but not yet) disciples.

Another group consisted of those who were merely curious. Rather than being followers of Jesus, they were followers of the crowd. They had come to observe the latest religious celebrity and discover what their neighbors were doing. They had not come to learn as much as they had come to satisfy their curiosity.

Among the curious was the third group, those who were supicious, those who were fearful that the teachings of this rabbi would only lead to more trouble. They had come with motives more akin to spying than to learning.

Jesus knew the most effective way to get his message across to the tentative followers, the merely curious, and the suspicious was to use an indirect approach. To address any of these groups directly would cause them to put up their guard. So he taught his disciples in a place where these three groups could overhear what he had to say. If they heard his message without being defensive, perhaps they would really *hear* his message, and in the process discover themselves being challenged and offered change.

When Jesus sat down, his disciples drew near and the crowd came in close to hear what he had to say. Although Matthew tells us that Jesus' teaching was addressed to the disciples, I am convinced Jesus was also intentionally speaking indirectly to all who had drawn near and were willing to listen with their defenses down. And, thanks to Matthew's pen, this includes even us.

"Seeing the crowds, he went up on the mountain, and when he sat down his disciples came to him. And he opened his mouth and taught them"[1] (Matt 5:1–2).

For Meditation and Conversation

1. With which group do you identify most of the time: the disciples, the followers, the curious, or the suspicious?

2. What do you know about yourself that may hinder your being open to the wisdom of Jesus?

3. What do you know about yourself that will enable you to be nourished by these sayings?

---

1. The translation of the Bible that is used throughout this book is the Revised Standard Version.

3

Blessed beyond Happiness

MATTHEW 5:2–3A

J ESUS LOOKED NOT ONLY into the faces of his disciples who had left behind old, familiar routines and relationships in order to follow him. He also looked into the faces and the lives of the others who had gathered near. He sensed, beneath their surface longings and desires, a deeper hunger. I suspect that many of them, like many of us, may not have been consciously aware of this deeper longing even though it was the hidden driver motivating much of their behavior.

In our society, this longing for something more drives many of us to exhaust ourselves trying to achieve and accumulate. It is why we worry and fearfully strive to protect what we have. I am confident that the people gathered around Jesus on that hillside were not very different from us. Jesus was aware that like us they too strived to make life worth living by seeking security in possessions and pursuing physical comfort and pleasure. However, Jesus knew that regardless of their sometime success in attaining pleasure, possessions, security, and comfort, these alone would never satisfy their deepest hunger. Within the heart is a longing for something more. It was this longing for something more that had motivated many of them to walk a long distance to hear what this traveling rabbi had to say.

Jesus knew this and began by talking about this "something more." He began teaching the disciples (and all who would listen) with a series of sayings that begin, "Blessed are . . ." Matthew's Greek translation of what

Jesus said can be rendered in English as "happy are," but only if one has a profound understanding of the word *happy*.

However, most of us seldom have anything profound in mind when we speak of "being happy." For most of us, being happy is feeling so good we smile and laugh because our best dreams are coming true and the world is not merely safe but also fun to live in. Although sunshine and flowers, laughter and pleasure are a very real part of life, the sun does not always shine and flowers are not always blooming. Life is not always fun. Sorrow, pain, injustice, and tragedy are realities each of us must face.

What Jesus was talking about clearly includes the sunshine times, but it also includes much more. He was talking about an all-weather reality. For most of us, *happy* is not the right word to convey what Jesus meant. It is not a word with enough breadth, depth, and strength to embrace and endure the agonies of Good Friday or the grief and despair of the dark nights of the soul that come on the Saturdays following all sorts of crucifixions, but before some sort of Easter has happened.

Whatever Jesus meant by the word we translate as "blessed," it is big enough to embrace crucifixion as well as resurrection, grief as well as joy, defeat as well as victory, the times that make us cry in agony as well as the times that make us laugh with delight. It is strong enough for the storm-filled nights as well as the days of beautiful sunshine.

Victor Frankl's experiences in a concentration camp in World War II led him to the conviction that the deepest human yearning is neither pleasure (as Sigmund Freud had said) nor power (as Alfred Adler had said) but rather the profound hunger for meaning.[1] One who is able to affirm there is meaning in life is blessed. Someone who can say with conviction, "My life has meaning" is truly blessed.

For Jesus, the source of meaning is God, and it is living in harmonious, obedient relationship with God that we discover both the meaning of life and the meaning of our lives, and find ourselves blessed by that discovery. This truth is illustrated in the life of Dietrich Bonhoeffer. He understood what Jesus was talking about in the series of declarations that begin "Blessed are . . ." Bonhoeffer was a promising young German theologian in the 1930s and early 1940s. His commitment to loving God and neighbor in the midst of Hitler's horrendously evil reign of terror led Bonhoeffer to go beyond his pacifism and work with those who planned

---

1. See Frankl, *Man's Search for Meaning*.

to assassinate Hitler and take over the government. The attempt failed. Bonhoeffer, who had been arrested earlier, was connected with the plot, and just before the end of World War II, he was among those Hitler specfically ordered to be hanged.

The way he lived in his situation and faced his death reflects the deeper meaning of "being blessed." On what was to be the last Sunday of his life, he responded to the request of other prisoners to lead a worship service. The two passages of Scripture he talked about were Isa 53:5 ("With his stripes we are healed") and 1 Pet 1:3 ("Blessed be the God and Father of our Lord Jesus Christ! According to his great mercy, he has caused us to be born again to a living hope through the resurrection of Jesus Christ from the dead"). Just as the service ended, the prison door opened, and there stood two men who were not in military dress. "Prisoner Bonhoeffer, get ready and come with us!" Bonhoeffer knew what this meant.[2]

It was late that evening when he was taken before a summary court. The next morning he was executed. Ten years later, the camp doctor who saw Bonhoeffer that morning wrote these words:

> Through the half-open door in one room of the huts I saw Pastor Bonhoeffer, before taking off his prison garb, kneeling on the floor praying fervently to his God. I was most deeply moved by the way this loveable man prayed, so devout and so certain that God heard his prayer. At the place of execution, he again said a short prayer and then climbed the steps of the gallows, brave and composed. His death ensued after a few seconds. In the almost fifty years that I have worked as a doctor, I have hardly ever seen a man die so entirely submissive to the will of God.[3]

The last words that one of the prisoners, Payne Best, remembered Bonhoeffer saying before he was taken to the court were, "This is the end—for me the beginning of life."[4] His confident faith in God and his commitment to love God and neighbor not only shaped the way Bonhoeffer lived his life but also the way he faced his death.

Many of us have known persons who have made tough and costly choices because their consciences were shaped by what was revealed

---

2. Bethge, *Dietrich Bonhoeffer*, 829.

3. Ibid., 820–21.

4. Ibid., 820.

through Jesus. They could not be at peace with themselves if they had done otherwise. The price they paid may have been the loss of their jobs and severe damage to, if not the destruction of, their careers, but their lives were blessed by the faith, hope, and love that shaped their choices. They lived confidently trusting that somehow, someway their living was making a difference in the sight of God.

Jesus would say it is appropriate to call these persons blessed. The blessed people Jesus was talking about are not only those who celebrate the joy of Easter, but also those whose confidence in God gives them unshakable faith in the midst of the darkest times to believe there is both meaning in life and in their lives. Their trust in the grace of God enables them to endure the agonies of contemporary crucifixions, confident that sin and evil do not have the last word. They are blessed not because they possess great courage (though they do) but because they live and die with great hope. It is because of this hope, this confidence in God and God's grace, that their concerns go beyond what is selfish.

The blessed persons Jesus was talking about are those who can say "yes" to life even while the world is painfully saying "no," who can celebrate the gift of life even while dealing with tragedy. They are truly blessed because regardless of their cirucmstance, they are confident that God loves them and that their lives ultimately matter even though the world may call them failures.

How does one become someone who is so blessed? This is what the Sermon on the Mount is really all about. This is the question Jesus began to address when he spoke what we call the Beatitudes.

"And he opened his mouth and taught them, saying: 'Blessed are . . .'" (Matt 5:2–3a).

For Meditation and Conversation

1. How does the blessing you long for compare with the blessing described in this chapter?

2. How is the blessing described in this chapter a gift in good times?

3. How is it a gift in bad times?

4

The Importance of Need

A S A CHILD I thought the kingdom of heaven was someplace above the sky where God lived and where people who were good and loved Jesus went when they died. I was about five years old when my great-grandmother died. I remember listening to my kinfolks talk about her enjoying a family reunion in heaven with all her relatives and friends who had died before her. I imagined her being hugged the way we were hugged when we arrived at family reunions where everyone was talking at once, retelling memories, especially the funny stories, and there was a lot of laughter. I could imagine them smiling, patting each other's backs as they walked inside where all the good food was.

As I grew older, my childish view of the universe was changed by facts. There really is no "up there" in the universe; there is only "out there" as our planet earth rotates and whirls around the sun in a modestly sized solar system among billions of such systems. My view of the kingdom of heaven became a little more sophisticated than a family reunion up beyond the blue sky—but only a little more. Drawing on imagery from science fiction, I imagined the kingdom of heaven as a kind of parallel universe where the souls of the dead went to be with God. But I still thought of the kingdom of heaven as a place, a piece of spiritual real estate reserved for the souls of the faithful.

Then it dawned on me: heaven is where God is. And where is God? God is everywhere, in life and in death. At about that same time, I dis-

14

covered that the word we translate as "kingdom" also means "reign." The phrase "kingdom of heaven" therefore means the reign of heaven, and heaven is where God reigns, so the reign of heaven is the same as the reign of God. In fact, what Matthew calls "the kingdom of heaven" is called "the kingdom of God" in the Gospel of Luke because in the early church these two phrases meant the same thing. Both phrases are referring to where God reigns in this life and beyond this life.

Persons are blessed when God truly reigns in their living. When God reigns in our daily living, we live confidently, trusting that God is for us and not against us. Trusting God, we experience the inner peace that both Jesus and Paul described as being beyond the understanding of the world (John 14:7; Phil 4:7). Because of this peace that comes as a byproduct of trusting God, we are able to let go of the past and be open to the future regardless of our present circumstance. One who can live in such a state is truly blessed.

So, how do we receive such a gift? What is the way to the kingdom of heaven, the reign of God in our lives, the special peace that is described as being beyond our understanding? This, in part, is what Jesus was talking about when he said, "Blessed are the poor in spirit, for theirs is the kingdom of heaven." What was he talking about and who was he talking about when he spoke of "the poor in spirit"?

At this point it may be helpful to take a little detour and consider the way the Bible uses language. It is the way all profound religious writing and speaking uses language; however, it is not the way a technician, engineer, lawyer, or medical doctor uses language. The way such professionals use language is one appropriate way. It is a way that serves the needs of technology. They speak what I call "flat language," using language to try to say one fact at a time and to say that one fact with absolute precision. We need to be able to use language with great precision. I certainly do not want to drive across a bridge designed by an engineer who was not very precise in communicating to the workmen the required measurements and specifications for steel and concrete. Nor do I want my lawyer, while writing the contract I have paid her to prepare, demonstrating that she can communicate a variety of meanings in the same sentence. I want her to use "flat language" in which every word is very precise and limited, its meaning as close to measurable as possible.

However, this is not the way that storytellers, novelists, dramatists, and poets use language. They use language in another appropriate way.

In their effort to speak profound truth, they push words to their limits, because profound truth is more than words with strict, narrow, and limited meanings can convey. When they write or speak, they use words and phrases like shovels loaded with levels of meaning—not like tweezers picking up one precise grain of meaning at a time.

The way language is used in the Bible and the way Jesus used language has more in common with a storyteller or poet than with a lawyer or engineer. Jesus' goal was to speak truth, not merely to convey some facts, and certainly not to provide a legalistic religious formula for manipulating God to do whatever we want. Some years ago, I heard someone say that the language of the Bible is like a layer cake: There is the top layer and then multiple layers beneath that. The surface layer is cake, as are the deeper layers. However, one misses much of the cake (and often a lot of rich filling) if one eats only the surface layer.

Now, back to the question about what Jesus meant when he spoke of the poor in spirit. Is the focus to be on the word *poor*? If so, the statement has to do with poverty of money and material goods, and the meaning is similar to the Gospel of Luke's version of this beatitude (Luke 6:20): "Blessed are you who are poor"—you who do not have a lot of stuff. When the focus is on material poverty, being poor in spirit has to do with living detached from any sort of materialism.

Or was Jesus' emphasis on poverty of spirit, being poor in *spirit*? If so, the phrase "poor in *spirit*" refers to those who are aware of their spiritual need, those who do not assume any sort of spiritual superiority. They humbly see themselves as being spiritually needy—poor *in spirit*.

Which of these two sets of meaning is the primary meaning? I am reminded of my father-in-law, who when asked if he wanted cake or pie for dessert always responded, "Yes." In describing persons who live blessed lives, Jesus was saying they are not attached to things (*poor* in spirit) and they are also aware of their spiritual need (poor *in spirit*).

To the extent that Jesus was focused on our being *poor* in spirit, he was speaking of those who live unattached to things. This type of poverty cannot be measured by annual income or the lack of it. What this statement confronts is our tendency to be in bondage to the money and things we have or to be in bondage to the money and things we do not possess but earnestly desire. The wisdom Jesus was expressing is that greed can distort our living when we lust after the things we do not have, as well as when we hoard what we have while trying to obtain more. Either form of greed is in conflict with the blessed life Jesus was talking about because sooner or later greed inevitably refuses to do what love and justice require. To avoid doing what love and justice require is to be in conflict with God and outside the reign of God.

Those who are not in bondage to things (whether they have much or little) are the ones who are able to receive the kingdom of heaven; that is, it is possible for them to live under the reign of God. For them, a commitment to justice and charitable mercy are possible because they are not in bondage to things they own or lust after. They are free to use their energies and possessions as God intends. They are quite comfortable allowing God to reign over the whole of their lives, which includes their bank accounts and stock portfolios as well as their calendars and schedules.

Because the *poor* in spirit are unattached to their possessions and free from the lust for more things, they are able to be truly generous. They have the freedom to give away what they have because they are not possessed by their possessions. The *poor* in spirit are free to live for a purpose greater than accumulating wealth and acquiring more things. As they strive to provide the basic necessities of food, clothing, and shelther for themselves and their families, their living is not dominated by either their lusting after more than they have or their resentment because of what they do not have. They are free to allow God to reign over their decisions about how they use their limited time and resources. Thus, they are free to serve the needs of others; that is, they are truly able to love God's children (their neighbors) and through that love to express their genuine love for God (1 John 4:7–12).

Paul Conrad was serving as pastor to a Mexican-American Mennonite congregation in Mathis, Texas, in the 1960s when I knew him. He was a carpenter by trade. Some years before, he had come from the congregation where he was a member (I think it was in Ohio) to that little South Texas town on a mission trip to help build a church. He and his family were going to be there for just a few weeks. But responding to the needs he faced, he stayed a little longer, and then a little longer, until that little South Texas town became his home, and the people among whom he worked became his extended family. He and his wife were able to give themselves to more than the construction of a building called a church. As they became aware of other needs, they gave of themselves to serving a community of people called "church."

At first he just filled in because there was no pastor. But in time he became the pastor of that Spanish-speaking Mennonite congregation. He and his wife left extended family and financial security behind in order to do what they could to live and proclaim the kind of love that has been revealed in Jesus. Paul and his family lived by a set of values far beyond what a financial statement can reveal.

One could make jokes that he was not merely poor in spirit but really poor, and Paul would not only have agreed but laughed. The truth of the matter is, in the very best sense of the word, Paul was *poor* in spirit. He was not in bondage to things and that freedom enabled him to live under the reign of God, responding to life and the needs around him, and thus he was able to do what he was convinced God wanted him to do. His was living in the kingdom of heaven because he was living under the reign of God.

Few of us are like Paul Conrad. In this life, most of us want more and more because we are driven by the perception that wealth gives us control of what will happen to us. And it is not only our desire to be in control that motivates us to center our living around money. The behavior of most of us reveals that to some extent we believe having the right car, living in the right neighborhood, having the latest high-tech gadget, belonging to the country club to which the "important" people belong, and sending our children to a "name" college will make us admired, bring us respect, and prove to the world (and most of all to ourselves) that we matter. Perceptions such as these seduce us to live in bondage to things. This bondage has led many in the United States to rack up extremely high credit card debt and to purchase homes they cannot afford. In our consumer and materialistic society, we are tempted to hock our lives for the sake of material goods and status.

Because we are so easily seduced by the illusion that our meaning and joy in living are inseparable from our material possessions, Jesus made the somewhat sadly humorous remark that it is easier for a camel to go through the eye of a needle than for a person with a wealth of possessions (a lot of stuff) to enter the kingdom of heaven, that is, to live under the reign of God as God intends (Matt 19:24; Mark 10:25; Luke 18:25).

But it is not merely those who already have some possessions to whom Jesus' words were (and are) addressed. He was also speaking to those who have very little. Jesus knew that we humans can be in bondage to things even though we may be living in poverty. He knew that merely being poor does not make us holy. Jesus knew that lusting after the things we do not have, thinking they will solve all our problems, hinders our ability to live under the reign of God. The extent of our bondage to materialism cannot finally be gauged by our financial wealth or our financial poverty.

When Jesus sat down to teach his disciples and anyone else who was willing to listen, he did not dillydally in confronting one of the major roadblocks to our living blessed lives: namely, our materialism, our intuitive belief that our worth in life is somehow related to the stuff we possess and the money we call "mine." Jesus said it is only the *poor* in spirit who are not in bondage to the things they have or desire, who are able to live the blessed life of having God reign in their living.

But Jesus was not just saying, "Blessed are the *poor* in spirit"; he was also saying, "Blessed are poor *in spirit*," that is, blessed are those who are aware of their spiritual poverty, who recognize their need for God. Sometimes our pride in what we have accomplished and in the recognition we have received causes us to be insensitive to our need for God and undercuts our relationship with God. When all is going the way we want, it is tempting to claim all the credit, to be insensitive to all we have been given and to live as though we are self-sufficient. This subtle form of egotism is not blatant rebellion against God; it is more like being afflicted with spiritual amnesia so that we forget whose we are and who we are. Little wonder we wander away from God, unaware that our lives are heading in the wrong direction.

I have heard some people talk as though being poor *in spirit* was the same thing as having low self-esteem. When Jesus said, "Blessed are the poor *in spirit*," that is not what he meant. Far from it. As a poster that was popular a few years ago stated: "God made me, and God does not make junk." The problem Jesus was addressing is that we are sometimes so proud of the fact that "we are not junk" that we forget we have been made by God. I think this is especially tempting when we have worked hard and achieved the kind of success that people whose approval we seek, applaud. In our pride, we all but sing the humorous song that was popular about the same time as that poster: "O Lord, It's Hard to Be Humble when You're Perfect in Every Way."

During my second year in seminary, I was asked to help lead a worship service. The preacher that day was Dr. Albert Outler. Dr. Outler was one of the most brilliant men I have known. He had earned worldwide respect among Christian scholars of all denominations as a church historian and theologian. If anyone really understood what the Gospel is and had a good perception of who God is, it had to be Dr. Outler. Just before we entered the chapel, he asked that we pray. He prayed a simple prayer that God would somehow use our efforts. Partly because of where I was in my infancy of faith and partly because I so admired Dr. Outler, I opened my eyes and watched him as he prayed. The man was trembling. And in that moment I caught a glimpse of what Jesus meant when he spoke of the poor *in spirit*.

To live blessed lives requires us to be able to see and acknowledge the awesome mystery of God and the reality of our dependence on God and God's grace. Persons who live the kind of blessed lives Jesus was talking about know they need more than themselves and more than their things. They are persons who know their primary hope is hope in God, the God of Abraham, Isaac, and Jacob, the God made known in Jesus Christ.

Because they rely on God, they live in the kingdom of heaven—that is, God reigns wherever they find themselves. Their living reflects the will of God; and because it does, their daily living participates in that which is eternal in life and beyond death. This is why it is appropriate to call them blessed.

"*Blessed are the poor in spirit, for theirs is the kingdom of heaven*" (Matt 5:3).

For Meditation and Conversation

1. What are the symptoms of your being *poor* in spirit?

2. What are the symptoms of your being poor *in spirit*?

3. What are some ways these two types of poverty have blessed your life?

4. What are signs that God reigns in your living, that is, what are signs that you live in the kingdom of heaven, the kingdom of God?

5

Strength to Love

MATTHEW 5:4

BECAUSE LIFE IS NOT all sunshine and laughter, Jesus addressed the reality of grief and how to deal with it as part of living a blessed life.

My first major experience of painful grief came when I was thirty. Dad and I had just begun to experience an adult relationship when he was diagnosed as having lung cancer. Ninety days later he was dead.

Many of my friends expressed genuine sympathy; that is, they let me know they were experiencing some portion of the sorrow I felt. Every once in a while, an expression of their sympathy comforted me. The difference between the sympathy and the comfort I received is the difference between others feeling something of what I was feeling and my being somehow strengthened by their caring so that I was better able to face the reality of Dad's death and empowered to move on with my life. This is the essence of comfort: to be given strength to face what must be faced and empowered to move on. To receive comfort in the midst of mourning is a great blessing.

I am convinced that when Jesus said, "Blessed are those who mourn, for they shall be comforted," he was speaking not only to persons whose mourning was caused by the death of a loved one; he was also talking about the grief we experience whenever that which we love is lost. When a precious dream has been shattered, there is mourning. When someone we love becomes entangled in a self-destructive addiction, we grieve because of the mess he or she is in, and we also are in mourning because of the loss of what could have been. When a relationship is shattered by betrayal, when a marriage dies, we grieve.

The mourning Jesus was talking about also includes the deep heart-ache we experience when our neighbors are caught in the midst of destructive situations. We can experience deep grief when we become aware of a child trapped in a family where anger abounds and abuse happens. We can also experience the mourning Jesus was talking about when our heart aches because of the injustice done to others. I remember going through the memorial to the Holocaust in Jerusalem with a group that included Kathleen Jones. Her grief over the injustice done decades ago brought her to tears. We mourn when we are aware that prejudice, or greed, or pride, or fear, or God only knows what is distorting and even destroying what is good and leaving behind an ongoing legacy of chaos and pain.

Toward the end of his ministry, Jesus looked at Jerusalem and wept because the people were so far from God while at the same time being outwardly religious (Luke 19:41). His tears were tears of grief; he was in mourning.

When Jesus addressed those who mourn, I am confident that he was including those who mourn because of the brokenness they see in life, the lost potential caused by injustice, the pain caused by insensitivity and greed, the harm that is done in the name of religion, and the injustice the powerful make legal with self-serving laws. Jesus, who calls us to love our neighbors as ourselves, was aware that when we love our neighbors, we mourn when our neighbors suffer.

My good friend, Chuck Merrill, who died too soon, was one who lived the kind of mourning Jesus talked about. He especially mourned the suffering caused by social injustice. He did not live with a sad face. He was a man of laughter who knew how to enjoy life, but when he looked out at the world and saw inequities and injustice, he mourned. I do not mean Chuck merely wrung his hands, feeling sorry for those who are suffering injustice. More often than not, his grief expressed itself in a kind of holy outrage. As a pastor, he talked about the injustice he saw, motivating others to focus on what needed correcting; and he did more than talk: as he was able, he was involved doing what he could to bring about change for the better. It was not unusual, however, for his mourning to be compounded by his awareness that what is being done to change what is wrong is frequently too little, too late.

The people who mourn the injustice and suffering they see in the world are persons of compassion. Their love for what is truly good (one of the ways we express our love of God) and their love for their neighbors leads them time and again into profound mourning because of all the ways the world crucifies the good, generation after generation. Because of the crucifixions they witness, they have a deep understanding of what Jesus meant when he cried out from the cross, "My God, why have You forsaken me?" (Mark 15.34).

Because love makes us vulnerable to grief, we are tempted to avoid love, to distance ourselves from others and to resist becoming involved in working for what we know in our heart is right and good and just. We do not want to take the risk that might lead us into mourning. We might be more involved with others and in working for what we know is good, true, and just if we could be assured that our efforts would not be wasted and that there would be a happy ending. But we know too much about the reality of all sorts of crucifixions. In fact, we are so aware of crucifixions in life, we tend to avoid becoming involved—not only because we want to avoid the sacrifice involved but also because we are afraid that our sacrifice will be wasted and accomplish nothing.

This kind of fear often makes cowards of us, and we fail to take the risks involved in loving our neighbor as ourselves and loving God with all we are and have. Too frequently we call this avoiding of responsibility "being realistic." However, this failure to say and/or do what we know in our hearts is right is really the failure to be the persons God intends us to be (the persons we know we ought to be). The more we are aware of this failure, the more we experience the grief that only sinners ashamed of their own sin can know.

When we experience this mourning caused by our sin, it is a sign that to some extent we have within us at least the desire to live our lives loving God and neighbor. It is this desire, this awareness of the way we wish we were, that triggers our grief when we have failed to fulfill our potential. Those whose love of God and neighbor is such that their failure to live accordingly causes them grief are also among those to whom Jesus was speaking when he said, "Blessed are those who mourn, for they shall be comforted."

When Jesus said, "Blessed are those who mourn, for they shall be comforted," he was using language in a way that reaches out to embrace all aspects of grief related to loving others. When we love our neighbors so much that we grieve their death, or when we love our neighbors so much that we are in mourning because of the injustice they suffer, or when we grieve because of our failure to live as the persons God intends us to be, Jesus tells us we will be comforted.

How does this comforting (empowering) grace come into our lives? More often than not, it is only in hindsight that we recognize how it came. God's grace empowers or comforts us in our grief in a variety of ways. For example, when our grief is caused by the death of someone we love, more often than not, we are comforted by the grace of God coming through expressions of love from friends and family. We also receive comfort through our God-given faith in the biblical promise of life beyond the grave and our belief that God is with us in this life, that we are not alone.

When our grief is caused by our awareness of the unjust suffering of others, what gives us our deepest comfort (that is, what empowers us to move on) is the gift of grace that enables us to embrace by faith the truth proclaimed in the resurrection: When sin and evil have done their worst, God still wins. We are aware of this good news because God has been at work in the deeds and words of others across the centuries to bring this message of hope to us.

When our sin is the cause of our mourning, God's merciful grace comforts us through the wisdom, words, and actions of others, enabling us to hear and embrace with joyful relief the words of mercy Jesus spoke to the woman caught in adultery: "Your sin is forgiven; go and sin no more" (John 8:11).

The comfort that comes through the gift and acceptance of forgiveness is more than mere reduction of guilt feelings. It is being empowered to pick up our lives in the midst of the consequences of our past behavior and to move on with hope.

One of the greatest mysteries is how God's grace somehow gives us the faith to believe and trust the good news of God's empowering and transforming grace that comes in such a variety of ways. It is in embracing God's grace by faith (by profoundly trusting it) that we discover we are given the strength to face whatever is the cause of our grief and move on with our lives.

When Jesus said, "Blessed are those who mourn, for they shall be comforted," he was telling his disciples and all who would listen that the various experiences of grief that come from loving others and loving God need not paralyze or cripple us. He was assuring us that the grace of God will come into our lives through all the camouflaged ways God's love does its work in our midst, and that through that grace we will be given strength to face what must be faced and the power to move on, both when there is something we can do to set things right as well as when there is nothing more we can do.

We who mourn because we have loved others will be comforted. That is, we will be strengthened and empowered. And when we discover ourselves empowered (comforted) by God's camouflaged grace embracing us, we are truly blessed.

"Blessed are those who mourn, for they shall be comforted" (Matt 5:4).

For Meditation and Conversation

1. What are the various types of mourning you have experienced?

2. In what ways was your mourning a byproduct of your love?

3. In those experiences of mourning, what are some of the ways you have been given strength to face what must be faced and empowered to move on? That is, in what ways have you been blessed by being comforted in your mourning?

6

Disciplined Power

MATTHEW 5:5

ONE OF THE KEYS to living the empowered life Jesus was talking about involves the discipline of what he called "meekness." Some years ago, in a seminar, I heard Carlyle Marney tell a story about a letter that had been found in Egypt. That story helped me understand what Jesus meant when he said, "Blessed are the meek." The letter had been written in Greek by a Roman army officer to his wife on their wedding anniversary, about the same time the Gospel of Matthew was written; so, it is safe to assume the Greek words used by both that officer and the writer of the Gospel of Matthew had the same meanings.

In that letter the Roman officer told his wife he was sending her a stallion as an anniversary gift. He described the stallion as being stronger and more powerful than any horse he had ever seen, as swift as the wind and full of spirit, yet so gentle a lady could ride on his back and children safely play beneath his belly. "It is," the husband wrote, "truly a meek horse." The Greek word we translate as "meek" that the officer used in his anniversary letter is the same word Matthew used in quoting Jesus: "Blessed are the meek."

When Jesus said the meek are blessed, the kind of meekness he was talking about is the same kind of meekness that Roman officer meant when he described the stallion. This meekness has nothing to do with being spineless or weak, nor does it refer to being timid or shy. The meek

Jesus was talking about are people whose strength is disciplined and whose power is harnessed, gentle, and humble.

Who are examples of the meek Jesus was talking about? Persons such as Mother Teresa immediately come to mind. But we do not have to look to such servants of God made famous by media attention to discover these wonderfully amazing people. They are all around us. Their meekness—that is, their disciplined strengths and harnessed self-esteem—frees them from the need to call attention to themselves. This absence of calling attention to themselves makes it easy for us not to notice them. But if we pay attention, we will begin to recognize them among our neighbors.

Within our communities are faithful women and men who are engaged in loving God by giving of themselves in service to those in need. Without fanfare, they put their abilities to work feeding the hungry, clothing the naked, visiting the lonely, reaching out to the outcast; and they also invest themselves in more than face-to-face ministries. They also address the harm done to individuals and families by systems and policies of large organizations. They understand it is not enough merely to bandage the bleeding feet of the individuals who must walk barefoot through the glass, broken by all sorts of social injustice; they are clearly aware of the need also to work with groups, city councils, and legislatures to sweep up the broken glass, and to prevent the breaking of more glass that will cut feet, especially the feet of those with the weakest voices and the least power—the poor (Matt 25:31–46). They do all this because once they are aware of the need, it is what they must do in order to be at peace with themselves and with God. For them to do less would be for them to turn their backs on their true selves and on God. As they see it, they are merely doing what is needed, what they must do in order to be at peace with themselves; their motivation is not that of seeking recognition or appreciation. These are the meek Jesus was talking about.

The strength of the meek is inner strength and selfless compassion rooted in knowing oneself, accepting oneself, loving oneself. It is the kind of love for oneself that makes love of neighbor possible. "You shall love your neighbor as yourself," Jesus said, quoting from Lev 19:18 (Matt 22:39; Mark12:31; Luke 10:27). This knowledge and love of oneself is not self-centered. It is God-centered. The meek are persons whose source of strength is their trust in God, their awareness of their dependence on God, and above all, their confidence and hope in God. They know they have been created by God with various strengths and abilities and the freedom to choose to use those gifts for good. They know their fulfillment comes only as they discover that what they are doing is fulfilling God's will. The meek Jesus was talking about are the ones who experience the joy of knowing their lives really do matter. In striving to live in harmony with God, they know that their focus is less on what they want for themselves and more on what God wants of them.

Living such a life requires discipline—spiritual discipline. The meek seek communion with God through prayer; they strive to obtain clarity about life and living through study; they celebrate and open themselves to God and God's grace through worship. In and through all this they are inspired and empowered to strive to serve God in all they say and do.

Sometimes when we humans invest ourselves in some type of disciplined living—be it the discipline required in sports, or the pursuit of business success, or being the ideal parent, or some other worthy effort— we become arrogant. We are so proud of our efforts and achievements that our focus drifts toward self-congratulation. We even begin to feel superior to those we view as being less disciplined than ourselves. This sometimes happens to us when we invest ourselves in spiritual disciplines. Obviously, such arrogance prevents us from being among the meek Jesus was talking about.

The meek are those who are not only strong and disciplined but also humble. Their humility is not a devaluation of themselves or their abilities. Their humility is rooted in their clear awareness of the grace they have received. They know it is only by the grace of God that they have their strengths, abilities, and motivation to live disciplined lives. Their humility is not focused on a negative view of themselves. Their focus is on the amazing generosity of God, their debt to God, and their dependence on God.

It is no wonder then that two other characteristics of the meek Jesus was talking about are gratitude and joy. The meek Jesus was talking about know that all their abilities, resources, and opportunities are gifts of grace. For the meek, thanksgiving is not a national holiday; it is a way of living. Because they are genuinely grateful, they experience the profound joy that is known only by those who are aware of both the gifts they have received and the love of the One who gave them.

Their living and serving is rooted not only in their awareness of all God has given them but also in their confidence in God. They know and trust God; therefore, when they face that which is more than they are able to do, they do not whine about their weakness. Nor do they try to get by pretending to have power or ability they do not possess. They do not try to get by on bluff and bravado. They are able to deal with the reality of their limitations because of their humble confidence in God. They know they do not have to do it all. The meek do what they are able to do and move on, trusting God with the rest.

Their confidence in God gives them confidence to face what has to be faced, confidence that is stronger than their fear of defeat or danger, stronger than their fear of evil and chaos, stronger than their fear of tragedy and death. They are alive with confidence in God. Because of their confidence in God, they not only move through their daily living enabled to be their best selves, they are also able to confront crucifixions with strength and calm found only in hope that comes from trusting God.

Jesus said the meek are blessed because they shall inherit the earth. To inherit something is to be given possession of that something. To inherit the earth is more than being given title to so much dirt. To inherit the earth is to inherit life. The meek, those whose living is disciplined by the love of God, shall inherit the earth in the sense that they will walk on this planet with neither arrogance nor fear but with the confidence of persons who know their place in life is a God-given place in life. They will walk through their days confidently trusting God regardless of the circumstances. They know their worth and their strength are from God, and they do not need to pretend to be important. They are truly humble, but their humility is rooted in strength, not weakness. Knowing their living has God-given meaning and purpose, they live without needing to justify their lives by proving, possessing, or pretending. Their appropriate self-esteem is humbly rooted in their confidence in God.

They move through life with a confidence in God that shapes their vision of life. They go through their days confident that God will enable them to face whatever has to be faced and empower them to move on. This confidence, this trust, this faith in God empowers them to do what they are able to do and to move on when there is nothing they can do. Because of this confidence and trust, their commitment to live as God intends is a joyful commitment rather than one of drab duty. The meek Jesus was talking about are those who so trust God that they are able to walk confidently through life, doing what is needed—enjoying good times to the fullest and not being afraid of or defeated by the bad times.

"Blessed are the meek, for they shall inherit the earth" (Matt 5:5).

For Meditation and Conversation

1. Name persons you know or have known who live a disciplined life of meekness.

2. What is the evidence that they are among those who "inherit the earth"?

3. What is the biggest challenge you face in living the disciplined life of meekness?

4. When you live the disciplined life of meekness, in what way or sense do you "inherit the earth"?

7

The Primary Hunger

IN TEACHING HIS DISCIPLES, Jesus talked about the importance of the basic yearning or hunger that shapes all we say and do. What is it we want most of all?

When I was a child, as soon as I entered a store with Mother, I would see all sorts of things I wanted. "Mama, may I have . . . ?" "Mama, buy me this." My children, when they were young, tormented me in stores with the torrent of their wants, and I have discovered my grandchildren have inherited this same disease. Only their wanting "this" and "that" is extended and intensified by the ads they have seen on TV.

To be born human is to be born a bundle of desires and hungers. The question is: Of all our hungers and desires, which one shapes our living? What is the yearning, the longing, the hunger that shapes our attitudes, influences our thinking, and motivates our behavior? What do we want—really?

Jesus said the blessed people are those whose living is shaped by their ongoing hunger for righteousness. The question is: "What is righteousness?"

For some, the word *righteousness* has less than positive connotations because in American English we often use it to convey something less than a compliment when we say, "He is *so* righteous." We say this when we are talking about the hypocrisy of someone who tries to hide his or her selfishness, lust, greed, and/or quest for power beneath the camouflage of appearing to be religious.

More often than not, what enables us to recognize this phoniness in others is that we know this territory well because we too have engaged in such a charade. Often it is our experience in being hypocrites that enables us to recognize hypocrisy in others. As children say on the school playground, "It takes one to know one."

This is my experience too frequently. It is not just that I try to hide my most base self from others; I try to hide it from myself. I try to camouflage my self-centeredness and selfishness in rationalizations beneath a facade of kindness or charity or piety. Even though what I say and do may accomplish some good, too frequently my motive has little to do with love of neighbor, much less God. All too often my pretense is so well done I fool myself so that I am insensitive to just how self-centered I really am. I do not think I am alone.

None of us likes to have our pretentions (especially those we use to fool ouselves) exposed. To a great extent, it was Jesus' correctly labeling phony piety as hypocrisy that got him into trouble with some of the religious leaders of his time. He saw through their pretension. I suspect that for many of them, if not most of them, their phoniness was so well hidden in the depths of their being that they were blind to their fundamental hypocrisy. In hindsight, I all too often discover how I have been blind to mine.

When Jesus said the blessed people are those who hunger and thirst for righteousness, he was talking about those whose ongoing effort is to live in a right relationship with God. He was talking about those who go beyond being merely a "religious" or "spiritual" person. He was talking about those whose living is influenced by their earnestly longing to be one with God.

I no longer remember the name of the biblical scholar who told this story. He was visiting in Israel when the car he was driving began to lose power, so he took it to a garage. The mechanic did an engine tune-up, and when he finished, he put down the hood, declaring in Hebrew: "It's righteous." It was a correct use of the word. He was saying the engine was in tune; all the parts were working in harmony; everything in the engine was functioning in a right relationship.

The righteousness Jesus was talking about is living in a right relationship with God, living in harmony with God. Jesus was not talking merely about behavior. He was talking about the relationship to and with God that shapes one's behavior.

When we aim at righteousness, behavior is one of the rings on the target; but behavior is not the bull's-eye. The bull's-eye is being in a right relationship with God. If we are living in harmony with God (in a right relationship with God), our behavior will reflect that. Righteousness has to do with our relationship with God, the ongoing process of living in harmony with God. When we are genuinely righteous (in right relation with God), then our behavior reflects that relationship.

Jesus said the people who live blessed lives are people who are hungry and thirsty for righteousness. What shapes the way they live is their deep and earnest desire to live in harmony with God, as God intends them to live. Because each day is a new day and each situation is different, those who live with a deep desire to live in harmony with God never reach the point where they can sit down and heave a sigh of relief at having accomplished the goal. The next moment, the next situation, is another challenge.

Fred Gealy was one of my spiritual formation mentors who helped reintroduce me to Christianity. His influence on me was not merely in what he said or did. It was in who he was. He is one who comes to my mind when I think of hungering and thirsting for righteousness; he also comes to mind when I look for someone who illustrates "blessed are the meek." As a young man, in the years before World War II, Dr. Gealy had been a missionary in Japan. When he was ordered out of Japan, he returned to the United States and became a respected New Testament scholar. He was also recognized as an outstanding organist with a vast knowledge of church music. When I was in seminary at Perkins School of Theology at Southern Methodist University, Dr. Gealy was in the twilight years of teaching New Testament and Greek, directing the seminary choir, and from time to time serving as the chapel organist.

If there was ever a man who could take pride in himself and his accomplishments, it was he. But that is not who he was. Dr. Gealy was the professor who helped students organize an early morning prayer service and was a regular participant. He was a quiet man who saw deeply into life, into the Scriptures, into himself, and into the lives of his students. He was a man of prayer. He was a man who chose to sit on a footstool in the living room of his small house so that his visiting students could sit in chairs or on the couch.

It was not unusual to see Dr. Gealy walking across campus, reading a book as he walked. I teased him one day, saying, "Is that the book with the answer?" With a shy smile, he said, "I keep searching. Maybe in the next one." With all he had accomplished in his many years of ministry, with all he knew, Dr. Gealy remained a seeker; he had not lost his hunger and thirst for being in tune with God, obedient to God. He lived with an ongoing hunger and thirst for righteousness.

The people who live the blessed life Jesus was talking about are continually hungry and thirsty to be in right relationship with God. No sooner do they finish one meal than they are hungry for the next. They continually seek God's guidance. These people are blessed because they pray, "Thy will be done," and really mean it. The result is, their living is shaped more by "What is needed?" than by "How can I get what I want?" They are aware of the bigness of existence and the smallness of themselves. They are aware of the complexity of life and the limitations of personal experience. Therefore they never see their goal as being people who know it all and have it all under control; they know such an accomplishment is impossible. Their goal is to be open to the guidance of God, to be always striving to discern God's will for their daily living. For such people, arrogance is an impossibility, and humility is just part of who they are. They are people who live with an ongoing hunger and thirst for living in harmony with God.

These people Jesus called "blessed" are sometimes accused of being unrealistic, dreaming idealists. However, they are realists in the most profound way. They are aware of the reality of evil and the temptations to frustration, selfishness, cynicism, and bitterness. They are aware of the reality of injustice and unnecessary suffering. They are aware that humans all around this planet live in societies so shaped by narrow self-interest that the people in those societies assume that employing cunning and power to take from those less strong is the way to live. They are painfully aware of what distorts and destroys life; and their awareness of such reality is a major factor stimulating their hunger and thirst to live in obedient harmony with God (righteousness).

Because the primary desire that shapes their living (their basic hunger and thirst) is their ongoing desire to live a right relationship with God, these people are always ready for a new communion, ready for a new bread broken for the living, ready for new wine in new and different wineskins. Their hearts and minds are open—open to new and different marching orders from God. They are not stuck in the past. They know what it is to live by faith—always by faith, never by formulas derived from what was comfortable yesterday.

Blessed are those persons who are always seeking God, whose search for goodness never ends, whose concepts of goodness have the vitality of the living Christ. They will have the satisfaction of finding fulfillment in God, of being used by God in ways old and familiar, and in ways yet undreamed of. They will experience the satisfaction of becoming the persons God intends them to be.

"Blessed are those who hunger and thirst for righteousness, for they shall be satisfied" (Matt 5:6).

For Meditation and Conversation

1. What are the characteristics of someone who hungers and thirsts for righteousness?

2. Whom do you know whose living has these characteristics?

3. Jesus said such a person is blessed. What do you think he meant?

4. When Jesus spoke of that person being being "satisfied," what do you think he meant?

8

Why Mercy Is Essential

Obviously life is not yet as God intends. There is need for change, for conversion from the way things are to the way God wants them to be. Wrong is done; injustice happens. Strife, discord, hostility, and warfare are part of life as we experience it.

We long for peace, and from time to time, one person or one group has the power of money or military or both to impose superficial peace on others. But peace imposed by force lasts only as long as the power imposing the peace is powerful. For there to be lasting peace, justice must be a reality between persons, groups, and nations.

In the midst of our complicated mess, how can such justice come into being? For there to be the possibility of justice where injustice has been so much a part of life, something more than justice is needed to get the process started; and that something more is mercy. Without mercy, justice is understood only as revenge (the "getting even" kind of justice), and peace is merely a pause between hostilities. This is true whether we are talking about bringing peace between persons, between groups, or between nations that have been at war with one another.

It is only in the giving and receiving of mercy that there is hope for lasting and just peace, because justice by itself alone cannot deliver lasting peace among people prone to sin. Both justice and mercy are essential for there to be lasting peace.

The mercy that is needed is the mercy Jesus was talking about when he said, "Blessed are the merciful, for they shall obtain mercy." What is this mercy that shapes the living of those Jesus called "blessed"? What is the mercy they receive? What does living a merciful life look like?

The merciful are those people who view life in the way Jesus did. They are more concerned about the good that remains possible than about the wrong that has already happened. "How often shall I forgive those who sin against me? Seven times?" Peter asked. "Seventy times seven," Jesus answered (Matt 18:21–22).

The persons Jesus called "blessed" are persons who are able to see more than what is wrong with their lives and life in general. Their sense of compassion prevents them from being sidetracked in the futile effort of trying to keep score and trying to even the score. Without denying the wrong done yesterday, they are much more concerned about the good that is possible today and tomorrow. Their focus on the positive potential is what allows them to let go of what was and enables them to move beyond the pain in their past. As they move through their daily living, they are more concerned with fulfilling the positive possibilities God sees than with getting even for the wrongs done to them yesterday, last week, or last year.

To be sure, it is important that we hold one another accountable for the harm that has been done. To be merciful is not to view life through rose-colored glasses, ignoring injustice or living in the illusion that we need no laws, police forces, or armies because we want to embrace the fantasy that if we are "nice" to everyone, everyone will be "nice" to us. Sin and evil are realities that distort and destroy lives. Laws, courts, prisons are necessary in this fallen creation. But laws, police forces, and armies cannot finally bring lasting peace. The most they can do is temporarily force some semblance of order.

But the cycle of sin and evil is not permanently broken by tough justice alone. Merely meting out harsh consequences for bad behavior will not bring lasting peace. Mercy is also required; the truth is, it is is essential. Mercy is essential because mercy is focused on the good that is possible rather than on the wrong that was done.

The people Jesus called "blessed" are those who in their relationships with others concentrate on today's potential for good rather than on yesterday's failure—be it their own failures, the failures seen in others, or the failure of life to fulfill all their dreams. This is what the waiting father did in the story usually titled "The Prodigal Son" (Luke 15:11–32). The father embraced the prodigal son on his return. Why? Was it because it did not matter that the son had wasted so much of his life and what was his? No. The father welcomed him home because the father loved him, and the focus of love is the positive potential in the person we love. The waiting father was focused on the remaining potential in his son and the potential in their relationship rather than on the pain and failure in the past. This is the way those who are merciful view life.

I am confident that one of the primary reasons Jesus called God "Father" is that he was aware that God's love for us is like the love that an ideal, perfect parent has for their children. Regardless of what we have done in our yesterdays, the focus of the Father is on the positive possibilities in the present and the positive potential in the future. It is not that the past is erased or the consequences of yesterday's behavior are removed. It is that the focus of love, the tender love that is mercy, is on the positive possibilities that are still ours.

The prodigal son was not exempt from the consequences of the choices he had made. He had used up all his inheritance. He could never recover the time and possibilities that were lost in his prodigal adventures. But he was given new possibility in the midst of the ongoing consequences of his prodigal adventrures. He could have a new life—not the life that could have been, but a new life in the midst of the consequences of his past choices. Redeeming grace would enable him to make the most of his new situation. He received mercy from his waiting father.

A father gave his teenage son a car, and a few weeks later, his son lost control of the car trying to discover how fast it would go. The son was killed, and the father declared war on himself. Although the tragic accident happened years ago, the father remains at war with himself. He still goes to work and is involved in civic activities. During the day (most days) he is able to function by staying busy to keep his mind off his son's death and away from blaming himself for giving the boy the car, for not doing something to make his son a safer driver. In the middle of the night he wakes, unable to sleep, and is tormented by a thousand self-accusations: "If only I had . . ." and "If only I had not . . ." Even in the daylight hours, it is not unusual for an element of self-contempt to foul the air and distort his relationships. There is little peace within his soul. "God may forgive me, but I cannot forgive myself," he said.

One of the biggest challenges many of us face is being merciful to ourselves. Being merciful to ourselves does not mean we no longer regret choices and decisions we made in the past, but it does mean we are able to face the fact that the past is past. Today is the new day the Lord has made. We are able to let go of yesterday and give ourselves to the opportunities and possibilities in the present. Only as we focus on the possibilities God gives us in the present are we able to let go of the wrong choices we made in the past and be set free from our bondage to our yesterdays. It is in this kind of embracing of God's mercy that we are able to be merciful to ourselves.

The merciful persons Jesus called "blessed" are those whose view of life is shaped by their compassion for others and for themselves. This compassion enables them to see the needs in the world. Not only do they see the needs, they care enough to do something. They care too deeply to ignore injustice, to be deaf to weeping, or to deny the hungry. Because they live their lives focused on God and God's love, these people are not in bondage to the cruelties they see or to the injustices done to them and others in the past. They are not chained to the failures and frustrations of yesterday, and they are not obsessed with the shortcomings and sin of others or of themselves.

These persons are blessed because they live trusting that God is more interested in present and future possibilities for faithfulness than in past failures. They remember Jesus' saying to the thief on the cross, "Today you shall be with me in paradise" (Luke 23:43). They remember the story about Jesus refusing to condemn the woman caught in adultery and telling her to go and sin no more (John 8:1–11). Those who are merciful judge life by the potential God sees in the future rather than by the garbage the world sees in the past.

Because by the grace of God they are somehow aware that the past is past and that the only hope is in the posititive potential of the future, a merciful outlook shapes their daily living. These are the persons Jesus declared will obtain mercy—that is, they will grow in their awareness that God is more concerned about their potential for faithfulness than about their past rejections of God's will for their living. The merciful receive mercy in the sense that their focus on the potential God offers enables them to live with hope, rather than resentment, despair, or guilt.

It is the merciful who shall obtain the mercy of lasting peace because their exercise of justice will be tempered with the necessity of mercy. The justice tempered by mercy is one that strives to eliminate the causes of injustice rather than merely get even. The justice of the merciful lasts because it is focused on positive possibility and redemption rather than on mere punishment or revenge. It is a way of living into tomorrow focused on the positive potential of the future rather than on the fears and angers rooted in the past. It is only as the cycle of revenge ends that lasting peace is a possibility. This is true whether we are talking about our relationship with others or ourselves.

"Blessed are the merciful, for they shall obtain mercy" (Matt 5:7).

For Meditation and Conversation

1. What does it look like to be merciful in the midst of our daily living?

2. Why is mercy essential for lasting peace?

3. Describe an experience when you have received mercy.

4. Describe an experience of you being merciful.

5. What makes being merciful a challenge for you?

6. What do you think Jesus meant when he said the merciful shall receive mercy?

9

The Way to Be Aware of God

MATTHEW 5:8

WE HUMANS HAVE TRIED all sorts of methods for experiencing communion with God. Some of us have tried ascetic lifestyles and have walked on our knees until they bled. With passionate energy, others of us have tried to storm the gates of heaven through good works. In zealous fervor we have vigorously attacked what we are convinced is evil. We have chanted for hours and remained silent for years. We have carefully constructed prayers seeking to gain access to God, and we have studiously avoided any reading of prayers because we were convinced that the only way to God is through spontaneous praying. We have tried to dance our way into the presence of God, and we have refused to dance in our efforts to earn the right to be in God's presence.

Jesus taught the disciples that it is those who are pure in heart who shall see God. What was he saying? Purity of heart has to do with purity of intention and motivation behind whatever we are saying or refusing to say, whatever we are doing or refusing to do. What makes the intention and motivation pure is love—the kind of love that has been made known in Christ.

When Jesus was asked what is most important in life ("What is the greatest commandment?"), he said we are to love God with all we are and our neighbor as ourselves (Matt 22:34–40; Mark 12:28–34; Luke 10:25–28.) When Jesus spoke of the pure in heart, he was speaking of those for whom the primary motive behind all they say and do is loving God and neighbor. This kind of purity, according to Jesus, is the key to seeing God, to being aware of God. This way of living is what the writer of 1 John was talking about when he wrote, "Beloved, let us love one another; for love is of God, and he who loves is born of God and knows God. He who does not love does not know God; for God is love" (1 John 4:7-8).

The word for love used almost exclusively throughout the New Testament is not what most of us Americans mean when we speak of love. What we are usually talking about has to do with feelings—romantic feelings, feelings of friendship, feelings of love between grandparent and grandchild. But as many know, the Greek word for love that Matthew used in translating what Jesus said is *agape*. *Agape* has more to do with behavior than with feelings. It is giving of oneself for the good of the other, whether one is in the mood or not.

Agape is the kind of love that responsible, healthy parents give their children. Parents do not give of themselves for their chilren's good only when the parents feel like it. And to say they give of themselves for the good of their children is not to say they give in to their children. "No, you may not ride your tricycle in the street. And if you do there will be some unpleasant consequences." The good is what is in the best interest of the child, not necessarily what the child wants or what is most enjoyable for the parent.

The pure in heart Jesus was talking about are those persons who strive to live giving of themselves for the good that pleases God, not merely good as society defines it. Society is generally willing to say we are good (or at least okay) if we do not bother or harm anyone, and society is really pleased when we do anything that makes life easier for the people around us. But true goodness is more than that. True goodness (love of neighbor) is in conflict with those whose behavior is taking advantage of others. In such cases, true goodness is usually less than welcome—especially when, in setting matters right, some people lose money. One does not have to live very long to discover that true goodness is often at odds with the priorities of the society in which we live.

One of the ways purity of heart expresses itself is in true goodness that courageously stands against what is wrong. But purity of heart is more than merely opposing what is wrong. After all, I can oppose what is wrong for less than good reasons. I can do it for profit or for recognition or political advantage (votes, for example) or some other kind of reward. When love (purity of heart) motivates our living, our focus is on the good that is needed rather than on the gain I can receive or the pain I can avoid by doing what is right. Purity of heart is compassion that focuses on the greater good for others rather than on what is merely good for me.

Purity of heart is more than being obviously religious. Purity of heart is more than our emotional response in worship (be it a worship service using ancient liturgy and classic hymns, or a praise service with rock music and no formal liturgy). The sad truth is that all too often, we humans try to use our worship as a way of feeling happy and pious while at the same time avoiding the claims of God on our living and God's prophetic judgment on the injustices in our living and in our society.

Purity of heart (living shaped by *agape*) expresses itself in true goodness that goes beyond the most rigorous observation of and obedience to religious rules and laws. Jesus said that the pure in heart who love God and neighbor would see God.[1] The more clear we are about what is involved in loving God with all that we are and our neighbors as ourselves, the more we are aware of how far we are from such a life. It is not that we wallow in some sort of pious self-condemnation for being less than perfect. Rather, the more we become aware of what is involved in loving God as God in Christ has loved us, the more aware we are of how far we are from fully living in the image of God (Eph 5:1–2).

Because there is so much that is wrong in the world around us and within ourselves, we are sometimes tempted to throw up our hands, saying, "What's the use? I can't beat them; I might as well join them." Little wonder so many of us have a tendency to place striving toward true goodness somewhere below looking out for number one on the list of priorities that actually shape our daily living.

Some will go so far as to make fun of those who speak of goodness. Sometimes this is because the words *good* and *goodness* are somehow out of fashion. But more often, the reason is that the world is afraid that true goodness is too expensive. There are enough examples of those who have done what is truly good being crucified in one way or another to support the fear that doing the good is not worth the sacrifice. Little wonder that we are not only discouraged but even afraid. When we are afraid, we are tempted to do whatever is called for in order to be secure, comfortable, and free from pain—even abandon anyone or any principle if there is

---

1. See Kierkegaard, *Purity of Heart*.

some expectation that doing so will reward us with some sort of security, pleasure, profit, or power.

Only confident faith in God and God's mercy enables any of us to keep striving to do what is good without abandoning the effort. To be able to continue the pursuit of goodness (purity of heart) in the real world where sin and evil are at work takes profound faith. We need a deep and abiding confidence that even crucifixion does not defeat God. In the real world, where there is all too much injustice, greed, and cruelty, it takes deep faith—strong and confident trusting that God's grace will ultimately win—to enable any of us to continue the quest for goodness. Only those who embrace the deeper meaning of Easter are able to face confidently the reality of contemporary crucifixions.

The various ways we humans experience injustice, rejection, and crucifixion sorely tempt us to try to protect ourselves from pain by wearing the armor of cynicism and narrow self-interest. Only faith in God's grace that goes beyond what we can explain or understand enables us to continue to strive toward that which is truly good on those Saturdays after some sort of Good Friday when the love of God was crucified, died, and was buried. In such dark times, the triumph of goodness can appear to be only a childish fantasy. Blessed are they who, even then, move on by faith alone, continuing to strive toward the good.

But it is not only bad times and experiences of life's injustice that make our quest for goodness so difficult. We are also easily seduced by the cheers and applause of the crowd. It is tempting to drift away from yearning for and striving toward the good as God sees it, and to drift toward merely doing the socially acceptable good deeds for the sake of approval, recognition, or perhaps a more tangible reward. Jesus said the persons who are truly blessed are those who continually seek the good as God sees it. They earnestly strive to have true goodness shape their daily living—not only when such behavior brings rewards but even when the cost is crucifixion. "Blessed are the pure in heart . . ."

Those whose living is motivated and shaped by striving to love God and neighbor (the pure in heart) are blessed because, as Jesus said, "they shall see God." I am convinced this is the way Matthew's gospel proclaims what the First Letter of John declares: "God is love, and he who abides in love abides in God, and God abides in him" (1 John 4:16). To be pure in heart (to have one's priorities, intentions, and actions shaped by *agape* love) is to experience the presence of God; it is to see as much as human eyes can ever see of who God really is. As the writer of 1 John put it: "No one has ever seen God; if we love one another, God abides in us and his love is perfected in us" (1 John 4:12).

"Blessed are the pure in heart, for they shall see God" (Matt 5:8).

For Meditation and Conversation

1. What do you think are the characteristics Jesus had in mind when he spoke of the pure in heart?

2. What do you think Jesus had in mind when he said, "they shall see God"?

3. Describe your striving to be pure in heart. What empowered your effort? What got in the way?

4. From your experience, what is the relationship between being pure in heart and seeing God?

10

The Obvious Children of God

MATTHEW 5:9

Jesus told his disciples that when we live in the world as peacemakers, we are living as children of God. Peacemakers are also the people Jesus called the poor in spirit, persons who mourn, who are meek, who hunger and thirst for righteousness, and are pure in heart.

But where in the real world do we find such people?

We find them wherever we find people who, having experienced the grace of God, discover God's grace shaping their daily living. Somehow, someway, these persons have discovered they are precious in the sight of God. Without understanding why, much less how, they are aware that the mess in their yesterdays has been absorbed by the mystery of divine mercy. They understand that God views their past as past and that what God is really concerned about is their present and the future. They see life anew, aware that God is presenting them with new possibilities.

Is this not what the cross and resurrection mean for Christians? To the faithful, Easter proclaims new life is possible, and the new possibilities really are *new*—not merely the old ones with a fresh paint job.

The persons who are able to be peacemakers somehow are able to receive this good news not as mere information but as the truthful reality of their lives. This awareness is what empowers them to let go of the garbage in their yesterdays as they face whatever they must face in the present. Of course, they remember their past because it is part of their history, but they are no longer enslaved by it. They are wiser because of what they have learned through their past, but they no longer live in bondage to the pain and problems of their yesterdays. They experience what Jesus was talking about when he spoke of the peace he offers (John 14:7).

When deep within we experience this peace, we are empowered to do the work of peacemaking. We do not become busybodies trying to repair people and trying to fix everything that is wrong. Rather we move through our world, allowing our living to be shaped by God's life-transforming love; and as God's transforming love transforms our living, God is able to use us as agents of transformation. That is, we become peacemakers.

One of the most remarkable peacemakers I have ever known was an elderly woman in Mathis, Texas, in the mid 1960s. Mrs. Baker did not have an easy life. She was crippled with arthritis; she was almost totally deaf. When she had discovered she was losing her hearing, she had taught herself to read lips. She had experienced heartaches in her marriage and with her children. Finances were tight, and she supplemented what little she received from Social Security by selling her homemade pies to a couple of eating places. Her daily living was shaped by profound kindness and a deep sense of compassion that would not quit. Mathis was a poverty pocket—a place where migrant farmworkers returned for the winter months. How Mrs. Baker discovered the needs of their families for food or clothing or medical care I do not know, but with some regularity, she would solicit money from Sunday School classes or clubs or individuals and then she would appeal to the compassion of store owners or the pharmacists to provide what was needed at no profit.

A favorite memory of mine is what she did when the town was split between the Anglos who had run things for years and the Mexican-Americans who had discovered their political power and had taken over both the school board and the city council. There were angry feelings growing out of the elections. Harsh words had been said. The town was sharply divided. The angry words and threats broke Mrs. Baker's heart (blessed are those who mourn). Rather than get on a soapbox and verbally blast the people on both sides who were acting in hurtful and destructive ways, she went to the city council to ask if she could plant some flowers in a neglected city park.

Everyone in the small town loved and respected Mrs. Baker. They knew she was not just a sweet old lady, but rather a person who had been there for them when they needed her. She had brought soup when they were sick. They had either been helped by her when they were in need or she had enlisted their help to provide for others in need. She had been a sort of mother figure for most of the men on both sides of the political divide when those men had been children growing up in that small, South Texas agricultural community. It was always difficult to tell Mrs. Baker "no" for anything she asked because she never asked anything for herself but always for someone in need. When she asked to plant flowers in the neglected park, her request was easily and quickly granted.

Then this sweet lady, as innocent as a dove and as wise as a serpent, went to individual men on both sides of the political war. She would say, "You know that park has really been neglected, and I have permission to plant flowers. But my old arthritis is acting up and I cannot do the digging. Will you meet me at the park early next Saturday morning to do a little digging for me?" No one could tell her no. None of the men realized she was also asking men who were their political enemies. On that Saturday morning, there was some surprise when men who had been engaged in the ugliest kinds of political battles with one another discovered that to do what they had promised Mrs. Baker, they were going to have to work side by side. But it was for Mrs. Baker, and none of them wanted it said that he had been the one to walk away from helping Mrs. Baker plant flowers in the city park.

Mrs. Baker was her usual cheerful self, appreciating their coming, bragging on their efforts. As the work was about done, the closest thing she said to a lecture or sermon was, "See. You boys really can work together." It would be nice to report that this episode ended the feud. It did not. However, the volatility of the verbal exchanges was never again quite as high as it had been.

Blessed are the peacemakers. These persons are blessed because, by the grace of God, they forget about themselves in their efforts to bring healing and wholeness. One of the reasons they are able to invest themselves so completely in working for healing is that they have peace within themselves, which is a way of saying they are able to love others because they love themselves. Their love of self is exceeded only by their love of God and of neighbor.

Peacemakers are people who have experienced God's healing grace at work in their own lives. They have known something about pain and heartache; and aware of it or not, they have experienced God's grace bring them a sense of wholeness—*shalom*. Because of the healing work of grace in their lives, they are blessed with a kind of inner peace that allows and empowers them to reach out to the need and hurt of others. This was true of Mrs. Baker. She fit the title of Henri Nouwen's book *The Wounded Healer.*

Because those who are peacemakers know about both pain (they mourn) and healing (they know about mercy), they are motivated and able to give themselves in serving the broken and wounded. They are able to take the risks involved in trying to tear down walls that keep people alienated from one another. They are persons who are willing to invest themselves in trying to reestablish communication through the rubble of war between people. They build bridges across the pain-filled canyons carved into life by rivers of pride and the all too familiar winds of prejudice. They are those who are willing to invest themselves in striving to make the various systems and institutions of society more just.

These are people who bring healing, wholeness, *shalom*—peace. They are people living in the image of God, striving to do the will of God. What would it be appropriate to call such people if not "children of God"?

"Blessed are the peacemakers, for they shall be called the children of God" (Matt 5:9).

For Meditation and Conversation

1. If you have observed someone being a peacemaker, how would you describe his or her characteristics and way of living?

2. What do you see as the correlation between being empowered to love oneself and being empowered to invest oneself for the good of others?

3. Looking back on your life, describe a time when you were the kind of peacemaker Jesus was talking about.

11

Who Are Blessed?

MATTHEW 5:10-12

IF JESUS HAD SIMPLY been a religious guru sitting on a hill privately enjoying the presence of God and encouraging others to do the same, it is highly unlikely he would have been crucified. The world is not disturbed by people who deal with all that is wrong by withdrawing into solitary spirituality. It is those who call into question established, unquestioned injustice, and those who identify selfishness and condemn it, who are most often crucified in one way or another.

Jesus said the way to blessed living is for us to care so much for the way God intends life to be that we will not settle for the way life is—even though our caring may bring us under attack. Faithfulness is not an escape from the world. Faithfulness is living in loyalty to God, whose amazing grace has opened our eyes to what is really important in life and to what matters from an eternal perspective. Because faithful followers of Christ trust God with their future in this life and in the life to come, they are free to embrace the risks of faithful living. Not only are the faithful concerned for the plight of the individual, they express their love of neighbor by working for a just society and the elimination of whatever is harmful.

The persons Jesus described as "blessed" are those who care so deeply that they are unwilling to sit quietly while others harm themselves and their neighbors. They are so focused on the positive potential God has given that they will not accept the comfortable status quo, even though they are rejected because of their efforts.

The persons Jesus said are blessed are those who, because of their confidence in God and their love of neighbor, are willing to confront customs, policies, and practices that are driven by socially accepted injustice and comfortably unexamined lies. Jesus was saying, blessed are those who will give themselves for the sake of truth and justice—even while others are doubting their motives and attacking their character.

Milton Boatwright was the mayor of Mathis just before the political explosion I mentioned in chapter 10. Milton saw the tensions building. As well as he could, he tried to bring together some people on both sides of that social-racial-political divide. The Anglos damned him as one who was turning his back on his own people. The Mexican-American leaders damned him as one who was trying to undercut their desire for political power. Because he was an Anglo, they were convinced that his effort to work toward some sort of cooperative arrangement was another Anglo trick aimed at keeping them "in their place."

Milton saw the political train wreck that was going to happen, and he did his best to enable representatives of both sides to work together. For his efforts, he was verbally abused and socially isolated in that small town. Even members in the church where he was active gave him little, if any, support; many viewed him with suspicion as one who was selling out to the other side.

"Blessed are those who are persecuted for righteousness' sake," Jesus said. Blessed are those who, in striving to live according to God's will, give themselves for the sake of truth and justice, even while others are doubting their motives and attacking their character. Jesus called these people blessed because theirs is the kingdom of heaven.

What is the kingdom of heaven? As I stated earlier, heaven is where God reigns. And where does God reign? Heaven, where God reigns, is not merely some spiritual realm beyond this life. God reigns wherever persons, in this life or beyond, are striving to live as God wants. God reigns where people put into action what Micah wrote, "And what does the Lord require of you but to do justice, and to love kindness, and to walk humbly with your God?" (Mic 6:8) Wherever and whenever this way of life is lived, there God reigns; and where God reigns, in this life or beyond this life, is God's kingdom, the kingdom of heaven. When we allow God to reign in our lives, we live as God intends, and, living as God intends, we experience the fulfillment God intends. Then, even in the midst of turmoil, we are able to experience a peace that the world can neither give nor take away. To live with this kind of wholeness, this kind of peace, is to be blessed.

Although at times we may feel all alone, the truth is we are not alone, because when we live allowing God to reign in our living, we belong to a fellowship with others across the centuries who have also loved the world as God does and paid the price for sharing the cares of God. These are the persons who are blessed because they have been set free from the eternal despair caused by a lack of meaning; instead, they experience the profound joy of participating in the eternal purposes of God. They are living under God's reign. And wherever God reigns, there is the kingdom of heaven.

"Blessed are those who are persecuted for righteousness' sake, for theirs is the kingdom of heaven. Blessed are you when others revile you and persecute you and utter all kinds of evil against you falsely on my account. Rejoice and be glad, for your reward is great in heaven, for so men [people] persecuted the prophets who were before you" (Matt 5:10–12).

For Meditation and Conversation

1. Describe someone you have known who was rejected or ridiculed because of his or her effort "to do justice, to love kindess, and to walk humbly with God"?

2. What does it mean to say "theirs is the kingdom of heaven"?

3. Has your effort to be a faithful follower of Christ caused you to experience similar rejection and/or ridicule?

4. If so, in what ways were you (are you) blessed?

12

Who Are the Salt of the Earth?

MATTHEW 5:13

SOME PERSONS HAVE BEEN so hurt that cynicism and resentment color whatever they do; they live with the infection of bitterness decaying their souls. For others, life is so bland and tasteless that they do not really live; they merely exist. Both need the kind of salt Jesus talked about—the kind of salt that flavored the life of Marcelus Brown.

Everyone called him Brownie. He was the foreman of my work crew in Kings Canyon National Park the summer between my graduating from college and entering seminary. We spent the summer clearing backcountry trails in the mountains.

But before I tell you about Brownie, I need to tell you where I was emotionally and spiritually as I went into the mountains that summer of 1958 after graduating from the University of Texas. I was confused and, in my confusion, depressed. A few years earlier, I had declared I would become a pastor, but that was no longer my goal. Although I still planned to go to seminary when that summer ended, my purpose had changed. Rather than going to seminary to become a pastor, I was going in the hope of finding hope and meaning for my life.

As June 1958 began, I was visiting the brother of my grandfather in California. Uncle Fred had retired from the Park Service. For some years, he had urged me to apply for a job clearing trails in the backcountry of Kings Canyon National Park. When someone who had been hired did not show up, I was hired simply because I was there and willing to work.

53

It was more than a half day's horseback ride to reach the work team with whom I would spend the summer. From early June to late August, our camps were several miles from the nearest dirt road. Our supplies were brought to us on packhorses. During that entire summer, our crew slept under a roof only four nights. The other nights, we slept in bedrolls beneath the stars, in remote forests near rushing streams that constantly sang mountain-water songs. Our lowest camp was at nine thousand feet, and our highest at twelve thousand feet. Our crew of six (four by the end of summer) was together twenty-four hours a day, seven days a week, all summer long. To state the obvious, we got to know one another well.

Brownie set the tone. He was a strong, gentle, caring man, much older than the rest of us. Prior to World War I, he had made plans to become a Pentecostal preacher. During the war, in France, he went through a crisis of faith different from mine and yet similar in many ways. He had come home disillusioned. He drifted, worked on ranches, became a racetrack groom, and then during the Depression he started working for the Park Service. He knew those mountains the way I know the house I live in.

Along the way, Brownie became a wise man whose faith was simple, but far from simplistic; it was profound in its simplicity. He was not the kind of man to talk about his faith, and certainly not the kind of religous person who invades the lives of others with a lot of church talk and Bible thumping. He only mentioned his faith a time a two in passing. He simply lived, taking care of us, helping us learn how to take care of ouselves in the wild, and teaching us how to do the work—and looking back, I see he was also showing us how to live.

I think he sensed something of what I was going through. He gave me space without ignoring me. He let me know he cared without smothering me. On the rare occasions when he used words, he would say simple things about how important his faith was to him. Throughout the three months we were together day and night, Brownie never became pushy trying to save me. Instead, with profound yet simple wisdom, he lived the Gospel in front of me and from time to time told me stories about his life adventures and, without calling it by name, his faith journey.

Brownie was one of those special people Jesus was talking about when he said, "You are the salt of the earth." Salt adds flavor, and Brownie's life, his style, his personality, his way of relating to me that summer added the flavor of grace I badly needed. He reawakened spiritual taste buds I had allowed to become dormant. That summer Brownie was for me the salt of the earth Jesus talked about.

Jesus was aware that salt can be used not only to flavor the stew but also in preserving meat. It can be used to keep the good from going bad. Those Jesus called the salt of the earth (the blessed ones described in previous chapters) are involved in preserving what is good.

I entered seminary in the fall of 1958. That was toward the end of a widespread religious boom in the United States. When my class arrived at the seminary at SMU, the dean urged us to appreciate the opportunity we had been given because for each of us who had been accepted, several had been turned away. About two-thirds of the way through my first semester, I was feeling some guilt because at that time I had no intention of becoming a pastor; nevertheless, I had been given a very generous scholarship. After wrestling with my conscience, I decided that since I was not sure I was going to end up claiming to be a Christian, much less becoming a pastor, I ought to drop out of seminary. Carefully, I rehearsed what I would say to Dean Marimon Cunningham. I had prepared what I thought was an eloquent declaration that for the sake of my integrity, I should drop out of seminary. After all, I was not sure I could ever be a "believer;" and someone who really believed "this stuff" ought to be given my scholarship.

I thought through various responses I would make to whatever the dean said in reply. But the dean did not respond in any of the ways for which I had a response. He leaned back in his chair, threw his head back, and laughed loud and long, as if I were the greatest comedian who ever lived. It was not what I expected. Finally, he leaned forward and with a warm smile said, "Jim, we have enough students here with direct pipelines to God. I think we can stand to have a doubter among us. Go on, now. And we will talk again next May."

At that point, I was so flustered, all I wanted to do was get out of his office. So I mumbled, "Yes, sir," and quickly made my exit. By the following May, I still doubted that I wanted to be a pastor, but I had learned enough, experienced enough, to know I had to come back. I could sense hope, even if I did not yet have a firm grasp on it.

Sometimes, Christians who are the salt of the earth function like a preservative. It is a rare month, even these many years later, when I am not aware of my gratitude for Dean Cunningham and his grace-filled response at a key point in my life—keeping me where I needed to be. His laughter of grace was the preserving salt my soul needed.

When Jesus said, "You are the salt of the earth," he was also aware that in those days salt was used in treating wounds. Of course, in an open wound, salt stings. When we live the blessed life described in the Beatitudes, we are the salt of the earth Jesus was talking about. People who are characterized by this kind of saltiness serve God by speaking the truth in love, by doing God's will, by working for justice, and by loving the enemy. In so doing, the salt of the Gospel gets into the soul-wounds of people—and it stings. This stinging makes us painfully aware of our sin and the decay in our souls. There is little thanks for the stinging work of salty grace. No one enjoys being made aware of the sickness, the spiritual decay in his or her soul. We humans resist being made aware of the damage caused by our selfishness, prejudice, pleasure seeking, arrogance, pride, ignorance, greed, apathy, laziness, and self-pity. Gospel salt is cursed when its stinging makes us aware of our festering sin. Stinging love is damned, even though the stinging is vital for the cure.

While I was in seminary, some of us were involved in various civil rights protests, marches, and sit-ins. In our class were a few African-American students, as well as some students from Africa. We were offended when the lunch counter at the pharmacy just across from SMU refused to serve these students. So, we decide to stage sit-ins to call attention to the racist policy of that store. The sit-ins were peaceful—except for the time the owner called in the pest control people to fog the interior of the pharmacy. The fogging was effective in breaking up that sit-in. But in time, we were back. Students from the law school and the undergraduate school joined us. There were some articles in the paper. Many heated words were exchanged. I would like to say the owner had a change of heart. He did not. He simply sold his store to someone who did away with the lunch counter.

Sometimes those who try to follow the ways of Jesus end up being salt in the open sores of society—not unlike the way Jesus was salt in the open sores of those who were making a mockery of the temple (Matt 21:12–17; Mark 11:15–19; Luke 19:45–48; John 2:13–22). But because we want everyone to like us, we, who are the salt of the earth, are tempted to give up our saltiness—especially the stinging aspects of being salty. When we refuse to be the persons God intends us to be, we are as useless as salt that has lost its saltiness. Then, rather than being the salt of the earth, we are merely grains of sand, waiting our turn to fall through the hourglass.

However, once grace has had its way with us, once we have been reborn as salt, we can never again be comfortable in the ignorance and insensitivity that characterized the way we were. Once grace has had its way with us, we know in the depths of our being that we are meant to be salt, the salt of the earth. We know we are meant to be persons through whom God's grace is to flow, flavoring life with grace, preserving what is good, and working to heal the soul wounds of the world.

One more comment about being salty followers of Jesus. Salt dissolves as it does what it does. Salt that does not lose itself doing what it is meant to do is worthless; if it does not dissolve, it is not really salt, and is good for nothing. The kind of salt Jesus was talking about loses itself while flavoring life with grace, preserving what is good, and being an agent of God's healing love. As our ego melts away and we give ourselves to loving others as God in Christ has loved us, our living begins to make the kind of difference God intends us to make.

"You are the salt of the earth; but if the salt has lost its taste, how shall its saltiness be restored? It is no longer good for anything except to be thrown out and trodden under foot by others" (Matt 5:13).

For Meditation and Conversation

1. Who has been the salt of the earth in your life?

2. Who has helped add the flavor of God's grace?

3. Who has helped preserve what is good in you?

4. Who has been a healing agent of grace for you?

5. What impact did each person have on your life?

6. Describe when you have been the salt of the earth for others.

13

Being the Light of the World

MATTHEW 5:14–16

"YOU ARE THE LIGHT of the world," Jesus said. He was speaking of those who are poor in spirit, who mourn, who are meek, who hunger and thirst for righteousness, who are merciful, who are pure in heart, who are peacemakers, who are persecuted for righteousness' sake. The people Jesus had in mind are the ones he called the salt of the earth. Through the choices they have made, compassion shines like light from a candle's flame. They are so possessed by the Light, they themselves become light— the light of the world.

In a previous chapter, I told a story about Mrs. Baker. She invested herself in serving those in need in the little town where she lived. She was stubborn in her efforts. When she became aware of children in a migrant worker's family with no shoes, and with the winter months coming, she would not quit begging and badgering those who could help until the children had the shoes they needed. Mrs. Baker did not do what she did as a way of proving to herself or anyone else that she was a faithful follower of Christ. She was not a religious show-off, doing acts of kindness as a way of attracting attention to herself and her faithfulness. She did what she did because her awareness of the need of some children would not allow her to do less. Grace had so invaded her soul that she could live no other way. And the way she lived was a light of compassion that shone in an enviornment darkened by insensitivity, prejudice, and self-centeredness.

This is not to deny her faults, her failures, and her sins; she was no more perfect than Abraham or Sarah.[1] Like the rest of us, she was a sinner, but she was saved and made whole by grace; that is to say, the love revealed in Jesus shaped her living and was reflected in what she said and did. It could not be hid, any more than the light that shines in the darkness. Mrs. Baker was among those Jesus was talking about when he said, "You are the light of the world."

When we live as God intends us to live, our living is a reflection of the love of God. It is then that we are among those who bring light to the darkness the way a candle lights the darkness of a tomb. But we can choose darkness. We can hide our light under some sort of basket. Sometimes it is a basket made of fear or laziness or pride or greed or some other straw of sin. When we do, not only does our light fail to illumine the way for others, we too find ourselves stumbling in the dark.

In our secular culture, some of us hide our light under some sort of cover because we are afraid that someone who knows our faults and failings will call us a religious hypocrite. Our fear of being called a religious hypocrite causes us to pretend to be more secular than we really are, less religious than we really are. In other words, our fear tempts many of us to hide our light under a basket; and when we do, we become secular hypocrites. Although secular hypocrisy is more acceptable in our society than religious hypocrisy, hypocrisy is hypocrisy; phoniness is phoniness.

When we live as God intends, our living reflects the light of Christ. Our light gives light when we serve as Jesus served, when we care as he cared, when we speak as he spoke, when we forgive as he forgave, when we suffer as he suffered, when we live as he lived—not out of any motive other than being compelled by faith, hope, and love to do so. It is then that the grace of God shines through what we say and do, and also through what we refuse to say and refuse to do. When the compassion of Christ is reflected in our living, people who have been in the dark will see his light in us and say with sincerity, "Thank God there are people like you." It was certainly not unusual in Mathis to hear someone say, "Thank God for Mrs. Baker."

"You are the light of the world. A city set on a hill cannot be hid. Nor do men [people] light a lamp and put it under a bushel, but on a stand, and it gives light to all in the house. Let your light so shine before others, that they

1. See the stories in Genesis 12 and the following chapters.

may see your good works and give glory to your Father who is in heaven" (Matt 5:14–16).

For Meditation and Conversation

1. Through whom has the light of God's love shone into the darkness of your life?

2. What had they said or done that caused you to be grateful for them?

3. What tempts you to hide your light?

4. What is needed for you to allow your light to shine?

14

Dealing with Religious Teachings

MATTHEW 5:17-20

To excel in tennis or some other sport requires more than focusing on the do's and don'ts of the game. This does not mean the rules and techniques are unimportant; it simply means there is more to being a good tennis player than focusing on the rules and techniques. Maximum enjoyment of the sport comes when the rules, etiquette, and techniques are so mastered they no longer require conscious attention, and one is able to be absorbed in the joy of playing the game.

The same is true of marriages. Marriages that are full of vitality are not the result of merely staying focused on all the do's and don'ts that are basic for having a good marriage. This is not to say that there are no rules for a good marriage; marriages in which the basic rules are violated get into trouble and, if left uncorrected, fall apart. But to have a good marriage that is full of vitality requires more than focusing on keeping all the rules. When the focus is on keeping all the rules, the relationship deteriorates into a drab contest of keeping score. Rather than living in a relationship full of vitality and spontaneity, responding together in love to whatever life presents, the husband-and-wife relationship becomes a joyless, stagnant journey through a quagmire of marital legalisms.

Jesus was aware that when our relationship with God is reduced to religious legalism, the vitality in our relationship with God disappears. The more we focus on the religious rules and laws that we humans have developed across the years, the less likely we are to be open and sensitive to the activity of God in the present. The more intently we focus on rule keeping in our relationship with God, the less likely we are to experience the vitality of living in a relationship with God shaped by grace and faith. When our focus is on keeping the religious rules, we drift into religious score keeping. Focused on rule keeping, our relationships with others are distorted because we keep score on one another, judging the goodness or badness, faithfulness or sinfulness of one another by how well we and they keep all the rules. A sure indication of our drifting into religous legalism is when we find ourselves looking down on others. Religious legalism also tempts us to keep score with God ("God, I deserve better," or "God, I am thankful I am not like those who do not deserve the 'good stuff' the way I do.")

These and other distortions resulting from religious legalism upset Jesus and led to the harsh words he spoke to the extremely religious people of his day. Little wonder the very religious people said Jesus was out to destroy all that was sacred. Directly and indirectly, they accused him of undermining the Scriptures—the Law given through Moses and the writings of the prophets.

Jesus was responding to these critics when he taught his disciples, saying, "I have not come to abolish the law and the prophets but to fulfill them." He was not telling his disciples to be less religious than these very religious people who focused on rule keeping, but to be appropriately religious. "Unless your righteousness exceeds that of the scribes and Pharisees," Jesus said, "you will never enter the kingdom of heaven." Living under the reign of God calls for more than legalistic rule keeping.

Jesus was not teaching his disciples to reject their religious heritage but rather to embrace that heritage at its deepest level—to focus on the profound meaning and purpose expressed within the rules and traditions. There is a place for the law. The basic do's and don'ts have had a place in life from the beginning. When God created us, God gave us purpose; that purpose is to love God with all we are and to love others as ourselves. Giving us this purpose also required giving us freedom, because love is meaningless when there is no choice in the matter. Just as staying alive is tied to breathing, fulfilling our purpose in life is tied to our living as God intends. Problems and chaos are the result of other choices being made by ourselves and/or others.

From the beginning, there has been the universal, unwritten law that we are to live loving God and one another; such love is the basic, fundamental "do" in all of life. Implied in this basic "do" are all the basic "don'ts." Do not give the love that belongs to God to something else. This is the primary point of the first four of the Ten Commandments. Do not misuse and abuse one another. This is the primary point of the other six. We are to love God and one another; this divine expectation covers all the prophets had to say about the necessity of justice, mercy, kindness, and compassion, and all their warnings about the consequences that come from ignoring these basic do's and don'ts of living.

Jesus did not come to do away with the law and what the prophets preached. He came to embody the truth found in those passages of Scripture. He came to show us that the law is fulfilled when we fulfill the purpose for which we have been created, not by legalistic rule keeping.

Jesus' life and ministry call into account those who substitute keeping religious rules for fulfilling God's will. Jesus demonstrated that life is more than rule keeping when he violated a legalistic understanding of one of the Ten Commandments by feeding the hungry disciples and healing a man on the Sabbath, that is, working on the Sabbath (Matt 12:1–14). In this, he showed us that the law is fulfilled when God's will is done by serving those in need.

Jesus was certainly not advocating a lifestyle in which anything goes. The life and ministry of Jesus call to accountability any who claim that fulfilling the purpose of life is accomplished by eliminating the "oughts" and embracing the phony freedom of doing whatever brings personal gratification. The cross never was and never will be an experience of personal gratification or pleasure. Faithfulness was and always is the willingness to do whatever must be done, endure whatever must be endured, for the sake of what is truly and profoundly good.

The key is the righteousness of which Jesus spoke. This is more than the righteousness of merely doing the correct deed. It is the righteousness of living in a right relationship with God as revealed in Jesus.[1] This righteousness is the life that flows from us when our living is shaped by the grace of God revealed in Christ. Righteousness has to do with living in a trusting, confident, harmonious, and obedient relationship with God. It is the life described earlier in this book as living under the reign of God. It is trusting and obeying God even to the point of enduring the cross. It

---

1. See the comments about Matt 5:6 in chapter 7.

is being able to endure the dark night of the soul, confident that there will be an Easter sunrise.

All this is more than merely obeying some rules, and it is certainly not living in a way that denies or tries to eliminate the basic do's and don'ts of life. When we live in a trusting, confident, harmonious, and obedient relationship with God, the byproduct is that we live in such a way that the most profound and basic "oughts" (what Jesus called "the law") are fulfilled. To try to live otherwise is to reject and forfeit the gift God continually offers.

"Think not that I have come to abolish the law and the prophets; I have come not to abolish them but to fulfill them. For truly, I say to you, till heaven and earth pass away, not an iota, not a dot, will pass from the law until all is accomplished. Whoever then relaxes one of the least of these commandments and teaches others so, shall be called least in the kingdom of heaven; but he who does them and teaches them shall be called great in the kingdom of heaven. For I tell you, unless your righteousness exceeds that of the scribes and Pharisees, you will never enter the kingdom of heaven" (Matt 5:17–20).

For Meditation and Conversation

1. As you think about yourself and the people you know, what are some examples of religious rule keeping that hinder or block one's ability to live in a confident, trusting, harmonious, and obedient relationship with God?

2. What have you observed or experienced regarding what happens when people reject loving God and neighbor as the fundamental law of living?

3. One of the fundamental temptations in life is to look down on some individuals or groups because they do not live the way we believe God wants them to live. What is the correlation between such an outlook and behavior that hinders or harms rather than helps them?

4. What are some characteristics of a life shaped by God's grace that fulfills the law and the prophets?

15

About Murder, Anger, and Broken Relationships

MATTHEW 5:21–26

JESUS WAS AWARE THAT we do not always get along with one another, and sometimes our anger or greed is so great that we commit murder. Jesus also knew that merely obeying the command not to murder one another does not cause life to be as God intends it to be. From his study of the prophets and his observation of the society in which he lived, Jesus was keenly aware that the murder we do with our hands is not the only way we destroy one another.

Failure to be as concerned about what is good for our neighbor as we are about what is good for us undermines true justice, distorting and destroying life. This failure is the basic explanation of why, on this planet of plenty, so many people die each day from causes related to inadequate diet and unclean water. Failure to love our neighbor as ourselves is the root of all sorts of physical and emotional pain caused by neglect and selfishness. Certainly, chaos, suffering, and death caused by war, terrorism, and abuse are signs of the absence of self-giving love for the good of the other.[1]

Failure to love as God in Christ has loved us does more than physical harm. It is what allows the virus of self-centered living to flourish undetected like a hidden cancer in our souls. Focused only on ourselves and what we want, without even being aware of what we are doing, we become

---

1. "Love" is defined in comments on Matt 5:8 and 5:43–48 in chapters 9 and 19.

insensitive to the need of others and unaware of the injustice we create and perpetuate. It is not surprising, therefore, that those who are harmed by our self-centered living respond with resentment, anger, and the longing for revenge. Their reaction to our sin lures us into sinful reaction to their sin, all of which adds to the chaos and pain in the world.

We humans are interdependent creatures, whether we are aware of that interdependence or not. We were created to bring out the best in one another; however, a sign of our separation from God and the way we were intended to live is that all too often, our interdependence brings out the worst in one another. How many adults are crippled in their ability to relate to others because they were starved of love as children? How many relationships wither and die from neglect rooted in self-centeredness? When our words and deeds are drained of concern for one another and filled with contempt, the consequences are hurtful and all too frequently tragic.

Jesus taught his disciples that not only were they to refrain from killing one another, they were to be careful with their anger and to avoid insulting others. Insults distort relationships, and distorted relationships are the catalyst of all sorts of warfare between individuals, groups, and nations. Insults done in word and deed are all too often the cause of hell breaking loose among us.

Our failure to love others as God in Christ has loved us not only causes harm to others, it also destroys us from within. When we are unable to love, we live in a kind of solitary confinement of the soul. When we block the grace of God from flowing through us, we become like a stagnant river that has stopped flowing.

Stagnation of grace in our souls is revealed when we enter relationships only for the sake of what we can get from others. It is then that our relationships are reduced to negotiations in which we bribe one another with smiles we do not mean and gifts that are, in truth, bribes or payoffs. When we are unable to love, our involvement with other people is like being in a market where we haggle over costs and expectations—transforming our relationships into little more than business deals: "I'll do this for you, if you'll do that for me."

The New Tesatment calls us to live lives of love, in which we give of ourselves for the good of others. This kind of love has more to do with compassion and ethics than with passion—especially self-centered passion, which is so focused on gratification of the self that the humanity of others is overlooked or even denied. When the passion that drives our living is self-centered, the consequences are destructive because self-centered passion treats other human beings as things, as objects to be used for personal pleasure or profit. Seeing and treating a human being as a thing to be used or even abused is a kind of murder—spiritual murder, at least, if not physical murder.

Passion that ignores the dignity and humanity of others is inevitably destructive. When this kind of passion is let loose within our souls, it devours the best in us; and when we unleash it on others, we set in motion a landslide of destructive consequences—sometimes doing harm for several generations. When such passion becomes blatant contempt for a neighbor or group of neighbors, it is a symptom that we have turned our back on God and walked away from the grace God offers. Then, we are the ones of whom Jesus was speaking when he said, "Whoever says, 'You fool!' shall be liable to the hell of fire" (Matt 5:22).

In the First Letter of John, the author said basically the same thing. Although he used masculine language, he was writing about women as well as men when he wrote, "He who says he is in the light and hates his brother is in the darkness still" (1 John 2:9). "If anyone says, 'I love God,' and hates his brother, he is a liar; for he who does not love his brother whom he has seen, cannot love God whom he has not seen" (1 John 4:19). As long as we are contemptuous of others, our acts of worship are empty exercises of hypocrisy. Our religious deeds, done in the name of God, bear rotten fruit as long as we view our neighbor with contempt. God created us not only to love God but also to love one another. Our refusal to love one another not only distorts relationships, it decays unto death our ability to love God.

The goal is the kind of reconciliation where justice and mercy mingle together to create harmony and peace. We may never reach this goal in some relationships, but we are to continue to strive toward it. So, whether we have wronged others or they have wronged us, the goal is to strive toward reconciliation.[2] The goal is being one with each other and with God.

Our society tends to be a materialistic one, and the more we focus on acquiring things (and keeping what we have acquired), the more difficult it is to live in harmony and peace with one another, because the more we are in love with our things, the less sensitive we are to the needs of

2. See comments about mercy in Matt 5:7 and 5:38–42 (chapters 8 and 18) and forgiveness in Matt 6:12–15 (chapter 25).

others. When our living is focused only on what we want for ourselves and the select few whom we say we love, our personal ethics are diluted by rationalizations that justify our way of living. "Business is business," we will say. Such self-centered living blinds us so that even when we are wrong, we imagine we are right. In our pursuit of self-indulgent goals, we are insensitive to the problems we cause and the harm we do. The result is that those harmed by our self-centered striving become hostile toward us, and we toward them.

Little wonder that our society, focused as it is on materialism and individualism, has become such a litigious society with courts clogged by an overload of lawsuits. Of course, there may be times when legal action is necessary as a step toward true justice. But we need to remember that even when going to court is necessary, courts can neither bring healing nor build a healthy society in which people live together in trust, respect, and cooperation. The most our courts can ever do is to decide who wins and who loses, to place the blame and to punish for yesterday's wrongs. Courts, necessary as they are, can do little to create a better future other than attempt to send messages that will scare potential wrongdoers, thus preventing them from doing specific kinds of harm. The most courts and law enforcement can ever hope to accomplish is to enforce a superficial order. For reconciliation, healing, and wholeness to happen, one must go far beyond what even the best courts can accomplish.

Jesus was aware that we do not always get along with one another. He was aware that courts are needed in a sinful world; however, he also knew that we humans have a tendency to avoid the hard work of striving for healing broken relationships, and that all too frequently we find ourselves driven by anger or avarice to strike out against our neighbor by running to the courts. Jesus knew that for us to move closer to being people who live with one another as God intends, we need other ways to deal with our conflicts than one that is little more than a set of legal decisions enforced by some sort of police power. As long as we choose to deal with our problems and conflicts by seeking legalistic solutions, we will fail to have the life God intends us to have, and we as a society will continue to pay a terrible price for our failure to reconcile with each other.

"You have heard that it was said to the men of old, 'You shall not kill; and whoever kills shall be liable to judgment.' But I say to you that every one who is angry with his brother shall be liable to judgment; whoever insults his brother shall be liable to the council, and whoever says, 'You fool!' shall be

liable to the hell of fire. So if you are offering your gift at the altar, and there remember that your brother [neighbor] *has something against you, leave your gift there before the altar and go; first be reconciled to your brother, and then come and offer your gift. Make friends quickly with your accuser, while you are going with him to court, lest your accuser hand you over to the judge, and the judge to the guard, and you be put in prison; truly, I say to you, you will never get out till you have paid the last penny"* (Matt 5:21–26).

For Meditation and Conversation

1. Jesus expressed anger (in the temple and toward religious hypocrites), yet we say he was without sin. So what is the difference between appropriate anger (such as Jesus expressed) and the inappropriate anger that Jesus condemns in this passsage?

2. What does the message in the passage imply for your daily living?

3. What does Jesus' message in this passage say to you (*a*) when you are the one who has been wronged, and (*b*) when you are the one who was in the wrong?

16

About Adultery, Lust, and Divorce

MATTHEW 5:27–32

WHAT SHALL WE MAKE of what Jesus said to his disciples about sex, adultery, lust, and divorce?

REGARDING SEX, LUST, AND ADULTERY

Regarding adultery, Jesus went beyond the Ten Commandments. He understands that the issue at the root of adultery is more than sexual infidelity to one's spouse because it is not merely the physical intercourse with someone else that degrades the soul and distorts the marriage relationship. Wandering of the heart is the primary problem. When we allow our imagination to be captured by lust, we are easily seduced away from marriage vows and cherished love.

Somewhere in the writings of Martin Luther he talked about the fact that none of us can keep temptations from running through his or her mind. Then he goes on to remind us that there is a difference between a bird flying over our head and one making a nest in our hair. Being the humans God created us to be, we will from time to time be sexually attracted to others, even when we are happily married. The marriage vows are not an innoculation that prevents us from being attracted to anyone but our spouses; however, as Luther might have said, when we allow passing sexual attraction to turn into lust, the bird is not merely nesting in our hair: we are building it a birdhouse.

At stake is more than legalistic keeping of marriage vows. At stake is the integrity of our hearts and souls. Jesus knew that whatever we allow our hearts to dwell on will sooner or later control us. We may not be able to control what thoughts run through our minds, but we do have significant control over which thoughts we dwell on. If our focus remains on the temptation, even though we say to ourselves, "That's wrong, that's wrong," it is only a matter of time until we will be worn down and give in to whatever "that" is.

As long as I focus on the temptation to eat that last piece of chocolate cake, saying, "I shouldn't eat it, I shouldn't eat it," it is only a matter of time until I eat it. To resist the temptation to eat the cake I must focus on a greater good—that of wanting to lose weight either for reasons of vanity or reducing blood pressure. It is only as I keep my focus on a greater good that I am able to deal with temptation.

When Jesus was tempted just before he began his ministry, he dealt with temptation to use his abilities to serve only himself by focusing on a greater good. He kept his focus on his relationship with God (Matt 4:1–11; Luke 4:1–13). When the greater good of a healthy marriage is ignored or forgotten, temptation to adultery gains the upper hand. When one is in the grips of lust, relationship with the spouse is undermined, weakened, and finally ignored—whether or not physical intercourse ever takes place.

Jesus urged his disciples to do whatever they had to do in order to resist being seduced by their temptations; therefore, he called for more than physical self-control. With this call, he was not asking them to deny that the body is good; nor was he outlawing physical pleasure. What he was calling for is integrity of soul and body.

He knew that when the eye is an instrument of lust, it is unable to see God and the gifts from God; when our energies are busily employed in serving ourselves, they are unable to serve God. When our focus is only on our desires or hungers, it is only a matter of time until we find ourselves like Esau—selling our birthright for a mess of pottage that only temporarily feeds our hunger. When we do, the basic birthright that comes with being God's child is lost (see this story in Gen 27). Thus, it makes sense to get rid of whatever leads us astray, to cut ourselves loose from evil influence, no matter what the cost, no matter what the loss.

REGARDING DIVORCE

In Jesus' day, wives were extremely vulnerable, with few rights and little protection by law. They could be easily cast aside by husbands, and in that society, this often left them destitute. We can understand Jesus' harsh words regarding divorce as an expression of sympathy for and protection of wives in his day.

But there was also something more in his objection to divorce, something more we dare not forget—even in our age, when divorce is socially acceptable. Jesus saw marriage as a commitment so special it is holy. When marriage is rooted primarily in romantic feelings and sexual desires, there is a tendency to put the marriage aside when the feelings change and lust for someone else captures our longings. Marriage, as Jesus saw it, is no mere legal contract to be declared null and void because of inconvenience and boredom. Marriage is a commitment so profound, Jesus could not see it ending, except as a casualty of sin, a tearing apart that tears down—a deep and profound tragedy.

There are times when divorce is an appropriate act—but when it is, it is like an amputation, and with the amputation comes grief for the death of dreams, intentions, and hopes that once were alive in the husband and wife. Divorce is the funeral and burial when the possibility of what could have been has died. I am unaware of any marriage that ends in divorce having begun with the intention of ending in divorce. Marriage begins in the hope and expectations rooted in love. When marriage fails, there is appropriate sadness about the possibilities that could have been and grieving about dreams that crashed and burned.

But God's grace has no boundary lines. Healing and hope are gifts of amazing grace beyond divorce. God's merciful, steadfast love is beyond religious legalisms.

Jesus nevertheless understood that marriage is not a temporary and conditional agreement. It is the profound commitment of two persons to be united in a way so special it is called holy. The failure of the marriage is but one more symptom of sin in the midst of the fallen creation. It is the failure of the marriage (not merely the formal recognition of that failure called "divorce") that is further evidence of our need for the forgiving, redeeming grace of God to be at work among us.

"You have heard that it was said, 'You shall not commit adultery.' But I say to you that every one who looks at a woman lustfully has already

committed adultery with her in his heart. If your right eye causes you to sin, pluck it out and throw it away; it is better that you lose one of your members than that your whole body be thrown into hell. And if your right hand causes you to sin, cut it off and throw it away; it is better that you lose one of your members than that your whole body go into hell. It was also said, 'Whoever divorces his wife, let him give her a certificate of divorce.' But I say to you that everyone who divorces his wife, except on the ground of unchastity, makes her an adulteress; and whoever marries a divorced woman commits adultery" (Matt 5:27–32).

For Meditation and Conversation

1. As was said earlier, Jesus did not take a legalistic approach to the Scriptures he read. This being the case, how is one to understand in a non-legalistic way what he said about sex, lust, adultery, and marriage?

2. Just as Jesus spoke in parables, he also used metaphors. What do you believe he meant when he said, "Cut off your right hand and throw it away if it causes you to sin"?

3. How do you relate the forgiving, redeeming love of God to Jesus' comments about divorce?

4. Jesus spoke within the context of the male-dominated culture in which he lived. How do you you think he would state the same wisdom in our culture today?

17

Swearing and Truth Concerns

MATTHEW 5:33–37

W HEN ONE PURCHASES A new car, there is standard equipment, and then there are optional accesories one may add. Jesus taught the disciples that truth-telling is not an optional accessory. It is essential for life to be as God intends it to be. When we trifle with honesty, life is distorted.

When the White House tapes forced President Nixon to choose between resignation and impeachment, the issue was not that he had made a mistake or been misunderstood. Oval office tape recordings revealed he had employed the power of the Presidency to keep the truth hidden about the Watergate break-in. When his lies and misuse of presidential power were exposed, he was not the only one who paid a price. Those who had supported him experienced profound disappointment, even disillusionment. Across the nation, feelings of betrayal fed a growing suspicion of government and increased the amount of cynical mistrust of public leaders.

When lies are presented as though they are the truth, a cancer is injected into the relationship. It is only a matter of time until the cancer is exposed, and the bridges of trust are weakened, if not destroyed. Even if the liars get away with their falsehoods, they discover it is harder to trust others because liars tends to assume others will lie as they have done.

There is profound wisdom in the ninth commandment found in the book of Exodus: Do not bear false witness against your neighbor (Exod 20:15). The version in the book of Leviticus commands that we not only refrain from dealing falsely with one another (lying to one another) but also that we not swear falsely in the name of God (Lev 19:11)

Truthfulness is essential for people to be able to trust one another. Trust is essential for cooperative, harmonious life in community. When deception makes an entrance, it is not long until trust makes an exit. When lies infect a relationship, sooner or later the relationship collapses like a house on rotted wooden piers.

Out of the rubble created by falsehoods, the viruses of cynicism and suspicion are set loose to paralyze compassion and cause the cancers of suspicion and selfishness to spread rapidly throughout the community. Lies that cause the collapse of trust reenforces the human tendency to live merely "looking out for number one." When someone's desire for profit becomes stronger than his or her commitment to integrity and honesty, then accurate statements are replaced by whatever pitch will make the deal, and financial reports are written to keep the stockholders happy and the bonuses coming. Accurately stating the financial truth becomes a casualty of greed and cynicism. This kind of lying undermines trust between people and the trust required for the economic health of the society. Damage to individuals and society as a whole caused by the failure to be truthful in business is clearly illustrated in scandals made infamous by the leadership of Enron and by Bernard Madoff.

When lies are exposed and trust collapses, the sense of community decays, and people fearfully watch their flanks. When trust is gone, even compliments and good news are devalued and understood to be merely self-serving, diplomatic gestures masking ulterior motives. Without trust there is suspicion, and where there is suspicion, there is a lack of confidence and cooperation; creativity is undermined. In an atmosphere of mistrust and "you better look out for yourself," fear and suspicion replace trust and peace of mind. When truth goes, suspicion comes; and when suspicion comes into our lives, it is not long until relationships break down and all sorts of fears are set loose. These fears sap energy and vitality for living—which is to say, death reigns.

Because this is the way so much of the world operates, little wonder that we find ourselves swearing by all sorts of things, and even swearing in God's name that what we are saying is true: "This time I really am telling the truth; honest, I am, so help me God." In this sermon, Jesus said, "Don't do that. Simply tell the truth all the time—twenty-four hours a day, seven days a week. Let your 'yes' be yes and your 'no' be no" (Matt 5:37).

Jesus knew laws and rules cannot bring vitality to relationships, much less societies. In this passage, Jesus taught the disciples (and all who would listen) that we are not merely to tell the truth; we are to be truthful—full of truth. The truth is more, much more than merely being accurate about the facts we tell other people. Being truthful (full of truth) only begins with not telling lies. Our living is to be characterized by the truth that is revealed in Jesus.

The truth Jesus lived was more than merely being factually accurate like the ultimate statistician or the ideal objective reporter. The truth we see in Jesus is the truth that is the way and the life (John 14:6). Jesus was God's truth about life personified. The truth we see in Jesus is truth-filled love—the love of God and neighbor. Living love that embraces truth, and truth that expresses itself in love, is living as God intends.

Jesus was teaching his disciples to live in this way when he told them not to swear using God's name or "on my mother's grave" or on anything else. His goal was for them to live the truth all the time. Jesus was aware that when someone says, "I swear on my mother's grave it is the truth," that person is also saying, "This time I am not lying." What Jesus wants is for us to live the truth all the time. When we live the truth, we eliminate the need to swear because our "yes" is yes and our "no" is no.

But what about the courts requiring us to swear that we are telling the truth? This is a sad reality reflecting the sinfulness of human society. Among us sinful people, lying is done with such well-developed skill that it is difficult to know when the truth is being spoken, and so we attempt to play "King's X" with evil by requiring one another to swear to tell the truth. It is a pathetic and somewhat futile effort to control the chaos set loose by lies.

Are we then forbidden by Jesus to declare such an oath in court? It is well to remember that Jesus responded under oath (Matt 26:63–64) and Paul swore in God's name (Rom 1:9; 2 Cor 1:23; Phil 1:8). Even God emphasized his promise with an oath (Heb 6:17). What about all this swearing? Is this evidence of inconsistency? Perhaps it is inconsistency of human speech but not of divine meaning. What is consistent is motivation, intention, aim. What is consistent is God's grace—the mystery of the unmerited love of God flowing into our lives. This is the amazing mystery of God giving Himself for the good of others. The implication in this is that whatever we do in truthful love of God and neighbor is appropriate. We are to use the name of God in the service of God; there are situations in which even swearing in God's name might be done. Jesus swore in God's name; Paul did also, and so can we—but only for the sake of serving the neighbor in Christ's name.

When the neighbor (who may be a representative of the state in the form of a judge) asks us to swear that we are telling the truth, it is okay. This is a way of being a faithful person and meeting the needs of a neighbor. But the follower of Christ needs to be clear that it is not his or her being sworn to tell the truth in court that causes him or her to tell the truth; this swearing is merely a gesture of compassion done for the neighbor's sake. Truth-telling is a part of who the true Christian is, and such a Christian needs no oath to bring it out.

What, then, was Jesus telling us when he told us not to swear? He was saying much more than, "Don't use *God* as a cuss word." His concern was more profound than language etiquette. His concern was truth versus chaos. He was teaching the disciples to *be* truthful—not merely refrain from telling lies. When this truthfulness is the way we live, we have no need to swear in God's name; our "yes" really is yes and our "no" really is no.

"Again you have heard that it was said to the men of old, 'You shall not swear falsely, but shall perform to the Lord what you have sworn.' But I say to you, Do not swear at all, either by heaven, for it is the throne of God, or by the earth, for it is his footstool, or by Jerusalem, for it is the city of the great King. And do not swear by your head, for you cannot make one hair white or black. Let what you say be simply 'Yes' or 'No'; anything more than this comes from evil" (Matt 5:33–37).

For Meditation and Conversation

1. In what ways is being truthful something more than merely stating accurate facts?

2. What is the relation between living a life of love and living a life of truthfulness?

3. Describe persons you have you known whose "yes" is yes and whose "no" is no.

4. What are the implications of this passage for the situations in which you frequently find yourself?

18

Ending the Futility of Revenge

MATTHEW 5:38–42

WHEN WE HAVE BEEN hurt, we have a tendency to strike back, trying to cause more pain than we received. I suppose we assume that if we do more damage to those who have hurt us than they did to us, then not only will the score be settled but it will be done with such intimidation that we will be safe in the future. Massive retaliation is not a new idea.

Some centuries ago, the Hebrew people proclaimed "an eye for an eye" type of justice; and it was an improvement. Balanced retribution, tit-for-tat justice, was to replace excessive revenge and massive retaliation. But when has an eye for an eye justice brought an end to hostilities? Revenge almost always triggers counter-revenge.

Jesus was clearly aware that in personal relationships and in relationships between social groups, we humans will never arrive at a lasting, cooperative peace as long as an eye for an eye justice is the road map for getting there. To end the futility of the ongoing cycle of revenge, we need a higher goal than merely getting even for the wrong that was done. Jesus focused on healing old wounds rather than on trying to balance the amount of damage and pain. Only some form of healing can end the cycle of revenge.

Jesus offered another way to deal with those who do us harm, those who tear life apart, those who tear down the good that has been done. Jesus saw that the way to healing and rebuilding is through our giving of ourselves for the good of others—even those who have done us harm.

It was a vision of peacemakers moving through life bringing healing to the world through acts of sacrificial love. Jesus used the metaphor that when one demands your coat, you should give him your cloak also. The extra mile is to be traveled. Sharing with those who have needs cannot be merely an option. For healing and hope to happen, we must engage in something more than old, familiar ways of being nice to friends and cruel to enemies.

"You have heard it said . . . ," Jesus said. "But I say to you . . ." Then he pointed to what he saw, and his vision of life enabled him to see more than what is; he saw the way life is meant to be. He saw hope for our everyday world, hope made possible by replacing our revenge with active redeeming love—the kind of love we see in him.

Paul described this way of living in these words:

> "*Repay no one evil for evil, but take thought for what is noble in the sight of all. If possible, so far as it depends on you, live peaceably with all. Beloved, never avenge yourselves, but leave it to the wrath of God; for it is written, 'Vengeance is mine, I will repay, says the Lord.' (Deut 32:35 and Lev 19:18) No, 'if your enemy is hungry, feed him; if he is thirsty, give him drink; for by doing so you will heap burning coals upon his head.' (Prov 25:21–22) Do not be overcome by evil, but overcome evil with good"* (Rom 12:17–21).

I tend to respond by saying, "This way of dealing with life is unrealistic." But is it realistic to place our hope in tit-for-tat kinds of justice as the way to bring healing to relationships, society, and the world as a whole? Such efforts have not worked thus far; nevertheless, we continue to repeat what has *not* brought healing in human history in the crazy hope that somehow, someway, what has not worked in the past will work this time.

Some may jump beyond what Jesus was talking about and ask, is Jesus telling us to do away with courts and prisons? Is he saying just be nice to people who rob, rape, and murder, and everything will be okay? Just send love notes to terrorists and all will be sweetness and light? Is Jesus telling us that loving neighbors who are doing evil means that we do nothing, but allow them to continue distorting life, destroying life, and harming others?

Jesus did not mean for us passively to condone neighbors abusing neighbors, because such behavior obviously violates the command for us to love our neighbor—both the neighbor being harmed and the one who is doing the harm. When we fail to do what we can to protect our neighbor from harm, we fail in a basic way to love our neighbor. Nor do we love our neighbor who is doing harm to others when our being passive enables that neighbor to continue to distort God-given life, doing harm to others.

Some of us, some of the time, are seduced by the illusion of attaining purity and holiness by not becoming involved in the messy pain all around us. We even view not getting involved as a virtue. When we do, we find ourselves living in some sort of dream world where all that is expected of us is to be sweet, gentle, and nice. But when we avoid getting involved and employing the tough love that from time to time is called for, we do not make life better; we only make it easier for all hell to break loose.

Self-righteous retreat from becoming involved or taking refuge in passive noninvolvement when harm is being done to others only allows evil to run rampant, and it does nothing to bring healing and hope to the world. What is needed is love that does not turn away, and love that can be tough as well as tender—the kind of tough love that delivers justice with the goal of redemption rather than with the intent of revenge.

When Jesus spoke of our turning the other cheek, he was not teaching us to be passive in the presence of evil just so we can live in the illusion of being pure and holy. He was telling us that in our involvement with others, revenge is not the way to justice—the true justice that brings healing to life. For life to be as God intends life to be, we must not strike back; striking back to get even is not the way to begin to bring healing to a broken relationship.

To be sure, for life to be as God intends, there must be justice; but the justice the Bible proclaims involves setting things right; it involves doing what needs to be done so that lives can be reclaimed and relationships transformed. Sometimes, the work of justice must be done using nonviolent protest as a weapon of change—the way Martin Luther King did. There are extreme situations when some find that the only way they can express love of neighbor in the midst of an evil situation is to participate in more violent action, as did Dietrich Bonhoeffer when he surrendered his pacifist position and decided to work with those who were planning an overthrow of the Nazi government, which required the assassination of Hitler. Compassionate, realistic action that addresses the needs of those who are suffering because of injustice is the way to justice. This was the motive that drove Bonhoeffer. This type of concern for individuals and groups is to shape the way we do justice—not giving in to the desire for revenge.

In these models of faithfulness, there are not only profound implications for the way we as individuals deal with those who have done us harm but also implications for the way we as a society run our prisons and deal with those who have harmed others and endanger society. In this fallen creation where sin abounds, prisons are necessary; however, warehousing criminals in prison is ineffective and inhumane. It may express some sort of revenge-punishnment for the wrong they did, but merely locking them away does little to redeem and transform lives; therefore, all too frequently, released prisoners return to crime. In our failing to redeem (transform) lives, we contribute to making life worse, and we fail to bring into being the kind of justice that makes society (our life together) better. Failure to invest tough love in prisoners, but merely punishing them for their crimes, finally comes back to haunt and hurt us.

Going the extra mile and turning the other cheek are not understood correctly if all that is heard is the requirement to give in to those who hurt you. Helping those in need is the way we are to live in this interdependent world. Jesus was talking about living lives of love, the kind of love (*agape*) that is giving of ourselves for the good of the other—even the other who harmed us.

"You have heard that it was said, 'An eye for an eye, and a tooth for a tooth.' But I say to you, Do not resist one who is evil. But if any one strikes you on the right cheek, turn to him the other also; and if any one would sue you and take your coat, let him have your cloak as well; and if any one forces you to go one mile, go with him two miles. Give to him who begs from you, and do not refuse him who would borrow from you" (Matt 5:38–42).

For Meditation and Conversation

1. What is the difference between justice understood as getting even and justice understood as setting things right?

2. What are examples of persons you have known doing what Jesus was teaching, that is, turning the other cheek, walking the extra mile, etc.?

3. When has your life been enriched by someone walking the extra mile with you? What impact did that behavior have on you?

4. When have you gone the extra mile for or with someone, what impact did that experience have on you?

19

Loving My Enemies?

MATTHEW 5:43–48

WHAT JESUS TAUGHT HIS disciples regarding the treatment of enemies goes against my basic inclination. Some passages in the Old Testament are more in keeping with my usual response to those who would hurt me—a harsh reaction, even cruel and bloody responses. To be sure, one can also find some admonitions to be kind, merciful, and forgiving in the Old Testament; but when I am frightened into anger, protecting whatever I call mine, I find the bloodiest passages in the Old Testament that seem to justify revenge more to my liking.

But Jesus taught his disciples to love their enemies, to pray for them. For those who understand love primarily in terms of warm, tender feelings of affection, such a teaching is nonsense. Misunderstanding the kind of love Jesus was talking about has led some disciples in each generation to try to deny their true feelings and to twist their psyches into some semblence of phony affection. But Jesus was not setting us up to play hypocritical, pious games. Throughout his ministry, Jesus condemned religious phoniness. His most damning "woe unto you" statements were aimed at religious hypocrites.[1] Throughout the four Gospels, it is clear there is to be no game playing in the kind of love that Jesus was teaching.

The love that Jesus was talking about goes beyond the illusions and confusions of emotionally defined love. The love Jesus talked about is the

1. For example, see Matt 23.

kind of love that describes God. It is the love that Jesus lived, the love that led him to the cross for the sake of all, the love he expressed on the cross when he prayed for God to forgive all who played a part in his being crucified.[2] Such love goes beyond the parameters of emotion and warm feelings of affection. It is a kind of love birthed by commitment, implemented by decision, sustained by will, and nourished by faith and hope. This kind of love has more to do with the deeds one is willing to do than with the feelings one is able to experience. This love is rooted in being committed to live in the image of God, the God who gave and gives of Himself for the good of others—even His enemies. This love has to do with decision and action rather than emotions. It has more to do with what we *do* than with what we feel.

We can see evidence of what it means to love one's enemies in the efforts of Nelson Mandela to bring reconciliation between the black and white populations of South Africa. When he came to power, after being held a political prisoner for twenty-seven years by the white South African government, it would have been understandable if he had tried to get even for the injustice done to him. Instead, he worked to bring about reconciliation and healing. "He chose to believe that by displaying dignity and by consciously withholding animosity, he could accomplish far more than he could possibly achieve armed with a fistful of ultimatums and threats."[3]

When Jesus taught the disciples to love their enemies, he was not talking about the sentimental notion that if evil is ignored it will somehow go away. He was not advocating the naive dream that being nice to those who want to destroy us will make them change and be nice to us. Jesus' enemies crucified him. His giving of himself for the good of those who wanted to harm him did not mean he gave in to them.

But how do we apply this model of behavior to our situations? For example, how are we to respond to the terrorists who have captured the headlines, especially since September 11, 2001? How are we to love these enemies who have declared their intent to harm us and our neighbors? When we love as Christ loved, we give of ourselves for the good of others, whether we feel like doing so or not—and regardless of who the other may be. To give of oneself for the good of the other does not mean giving

---

2. See definition of love in comments about Matthew 5:8 (chapter 9).

3. Aikman, *Great Souls*, 123.

in to the other. Parents who love their children do not give in to whatever their children want.

When we love others as Christ has loved us, we are engaged in doing whatever is called for that will enable the other to become the person God created her or him to be. There are times this includes very tough love that says "no" to destructive attitudes and behavior. Doing what is good for others may even require tough love in the form of force—such as the force involved in keeping persons from harming themselves, or the force involved in preventing someone from harming others.

This truth presents faithful persons with difficult choices. As mentioned earlier, Dietrich Bonhoeffer's understanding of what it meant to love his neighbor as himself moved him from pacifism to work with those who planned the assassination of Hitler and the overthrow of the Nazi government.[4] Because evil—that which distorts and destroys life—is at work in the world, some persons give of themselves for the good of others through police work or military service. Because of the complexity of international realities, Christians have struggled and continue to struggle to discern when war is justified.[5]

Tough love takes great effort, persistence, and patience to deal with frustrations and failures. It requires the humility of being able to admit error and the willingness to modify strategy in pursuit of the goal of loving, the goal of giving oneself for the good of the other—especially the other who is an enemy.

What enables individuals to give of themselves for the good of others is the confidence that the resurrection of Jesus means that sin and evil do not have the last word, that God finally wins. It is this hope—the confident expectation that God's will ultimately triumphs—that empowers one to love one's enemies.

Such love not only endures the hate that comes from others; this love we receive through Christ overcomes our temptation to return hate for hate, because when God's grace controls our living, amazing things begin to happen within us and through us and, at times, even to our enemy. Anger is healed when life is lived with an awareness of and a focus on God's grace. Then the churning gut is stilled by God's gift of a strange inner peace that the world does not understand (John 14:27).

4. For the story of Bonhoeffer's struggle, see Bethge, *Dietrich Bonhoeffer*.

5. A good resource for exploring this issue more thoroughly is *War: A Primer for Christians*, by Joseph L. Allen.

There is no mistaking the family of those who love their enemies, because they are like their Father who distributes his love without regard for its return. These children of God strive to be like their Father, the One who is known by self-giving love offered both to the just and unjust. "Be like our Father," Jesus taught all who would listen, "loving even your enemies." In teaching his disciples to love even their enemies, he was teaching them to live as God intended them to live—in the image of God. Whatever else living in the image of God means, it certainly means that the self-giving love that is at the heart of all God does, is also to be at the heart of all we do.

When it is, we are, as Jesus put it, "perfect as your heavenly Father is perfect." This perfecton is not the perfection of flawless deeds and decisions without error, and action that never mistakenly does harm, but the perfection of flawless intention.

"You have heard that it was said, 'You shall love your neighbor and hate your enemy.' But I say to you, love your enemies and pray for those who persecute you, so that you may be sons [children] *of your Father who is in heaven; for He makes His sun rise on the evil and on the good, and sends rain on the just and on the unjust. For if you love those who love you, what reward have you? Do not even the tax collectors do the same? And if you salute only your brethren, what more are you doing than others? Do not even the Gentiles do the same? You, therefore, must be perfect, as your heavenly Father is perfect"* (Matt 5:43–48).

For Meditation and Coversation

1. What do you think is involved in loving one's enemies?

2. What is an example of someone loving an enemy?

3. Who are (or have been) your enemies? Whom do you find it a challenge to love, and how have you dealt with them?

4. What do you think Jesus meant when he said, "Be perfect, as your heavenly Father is perfect"?

5. What do you think he did not mean?

20

Misplaced Focus

MATTHEW 6:1–4

"Daddy, look at me!" The little girl was on the diving board about to jump into the deep end of the pool. It was not enough merely to enjoy the thrill and pleasure of jumping off the diving board into deep water; she wanted to be noticed by her daddy and to hear his approval and cheers.

Jesus warned his disciples regarding the dangers of being a show-off. Yet we all want recognition. As adults, in less overt ways, we cry out to those around us, especially those important to us, "Look at me!" It is very human to want approval from others, applause for our perfomances, recognition for our efforts, and rewards for our accomplishments. I suppose it is one way that we try to justify our existence and obtain confirmation that we matter. Deep within us is the longing to have others verify that we really are special and important.

At the beginning of his famous *Confessions*, Augustine wrote, "You [God] have made us for yourself, and our heart is restless until it rests in You."[1] One symptom of this restlessness, or hunger deep within us, is our striving to achieve and accumulate in an effort to demonstrate that we matter. From the outlandish hairstyles of rebellious youth to the workaholic efforts of adults trying to be a success, we are driven by the desire to be somebody special. Whether or not we are aware of this drive deep

1. Augustine, *Confessions*, 3.

within, it is a symptom of the restlessness of our souls reaching out for God. After all, we are already special—special to God; however, it is only in relationship with God that we are able appropriately to embrace our specialness. Jesus said each of us is so important to God that God knows all there is to know about us, or as Jesus put it, "Even the hairs on your head are all counted" (Matt 10:30).

Each person is known by God and matters to God. This awesome truth is hard for many of us to grasp—even more difficult to comprehend than quantum mechanics' string theory. It is not easy to believe that the Great Mystery behind and beyond all that is—the One some called Yahweh, others called Elohim, and we today call God—really knows us individually. What is more mind-boggling is that this One, who created this universe with billions of galaxies and billions of stars in each galaxy, really does care about each one of us. It takes a leap of faith to discover that the way to meaning and fulfillment is trusting this ineffable One, who is beyond our ability to comprehend and whom Jesus taught his followers to call Father.

Because it is difficult for us to believe such an affirmation, we seek to make our lives meaningful by achieving the recognition and rewards that the secular community or the religious community can give. We want people around us to confirm that we are persons of worth. Longing to matter in the eyes of others, as a way of making our lives meaningful, can lead us to engage in various forms of religious pretension. Jesus was especially hard on the conspicuous religious hypocrites—those show-offs who pretended to be more faithful than they really were. But as I stated earlier, there is another form of hypocrisy: the hypocrisy of being a secular show-off, pretending to be less faithful and more secular than one really is. This "secular hypocrisy" may be more socially acceptable in much of the United States and Europe, but it is no less phony than religious hypocrisy.

Jesus warned the disciples regarding the danger of being a show-off. One cannot be a show-off *and* a servant of God. One cannot be a seeker of glory and at the same time clearly focused on serving God and neighbor. The helpful deeds we do in the hope of receiving a reward or out of educated self-interest (a sophisticated form of selfishness) obviously benefit those in need, but they seldom help us in our relationship with God, because too frequently they are not expressions of love of God or neighbor. Because these deeds accomplish some good, they really are good deeds, and yet when the intention is self-centered, the motive is a reflection of separation from God more than an expression of faith and love. And separation from God is one of the classic ways to define sin.

It is easy for us to focus on congratulating ourselves; then, like Little Jack Horner in the nursery rhyme, we take pride in what we call our goodness. This is especially true when our self-centered efforts of charity bring us the praise we long for. But such praise tends only to make us hungry for more recognition, flattery, and honor. We go on doing good; however, it is not for the sake of meeting the need of others as much as for what we get out of it—momentary feelings of virtue and the recognition that our virtue brings us. Focused on our own sense of virtue, our pride makes us insensitive to our separation from God and our need for redemption.

Pride in our virtue leads us to believe any recognition and appreciation we receive is our due. When those who benefit from our helpful deeds fail to be appropriately grateful, perhaps even criticizing the way we helped, we feel justified in withdrawing from their need, halting our good works, and complaining about their lack of appropriate gratitude. Good deeds done for applause of some sort are done only as long as the applause lasts. Good deeds done from self-interest are done only as long as it appears that self-interest is being served.

Meanwhile, what happens to love of God and neighbor? This love becomes distorted and lost in the self-centered quest for recognition and gratitude. Those to whom this happens drift, bit by bit, farther and farther away from the life God intends them to live.

In this sermon, Jesus was telling his disciples that it is best not to make much fuss in doing good. Just do it for the sake of God's glory, he was telling us; do it for the sake of the neighbor's need and love for the neighbor. Do it, and be done. No need for audience approval. No need for some authority's reward. Others may see and applaud; others may see and be inspired; others may see and be outraged, but what others may see is really beside the point.

Jesus was telling his disciples and those who would listen that sin can be so subtle that even deeds that accomplish some good for others can increase our separation from God. "Beware," Jesus was saying. "Beware of being a religious, do-good show-off. Those whose deeds and gifts of charity spring from selfish motives miss what God has to offer—living with God now and forever."

"Beware of practicing your piety before men [people] in order to be seen by them; for then you will have no reward from your Father who is in heaven. Thus, when you give alms, sound no trumpet before you, as the hypocrites do in the synagogues and in the streets, that they may be praised by men [people]. Truly, I say to you, they have their reward. But when you give alms, do not let your left hand know what your right hand is doing, so that your alms may be in secret; and your Father who sees in secret will reward you" (Matt 6:1–4).

For Meditation and Conversation

1. Describe the behavior of people you know who have selflessly given of themselves for the good of others with no apparent concern for recognition or appreciation.

2. What do you think makes it difficult to put aside the desire for recognition, reward, or appreciation?

3. What forms of hypocrisy are most tempting to you? What lures you into that type of hypocrisy?

4. What inspires and motivates you to give of yourself for the good of others regardless of the response by onlookers?

21

Prayer and Religious Pretension

MATTHEW 6:5–8

WHATEVER OUR FORM OR style of praying may be, genuine prayer is being open *with* God in order to be open *to* God.

Being open *with* God involves being totally honest with God. If what I really want, more than anything else, is a little red wagon, I may say, "thy will be done," but the truth is I am not really interested in God's will; I want that little red wagon. When my heart is captured by desire for that little red wagon, my saying, "thy will be done" is phony. My true prayer—unspoken, perhaps not even thought—is, "God, please help me get that little red wagon."

My phony "thy will be done" does not fool God, but it can fool me into believing I am able to manipulate God with insincere words—especially if somehow I get that little red wagon. Rather than being more open to God, I am more committed to the illusion that I can manipulate God into doing what I want and giving me what I want. Rather than seeing prayer as a resource to bring my life in harmony with God's will, I embrace the pious pretension that the right kind of praying can get God to do my will.

One of the subtle temptations religious people face is the temptation to believe that by saying the right words in the right way while experiencing the right kind of emotion, they are able to get God to give them what they want.

Sometimes those who pray this way are not trying to manipulate God as much as they are trying to fool other people. They want others to perceive them as being persons of deep and profound faith; so, they work to create that image. Without making an intentional choice, their primary motivation in public prayer shifts from striving to help people experience communion with God to striving for approval and blessing from the audience. Even in private prayer, the focus can drift away from communion with God to concerns about saying the right words in the right way. It is easy for prayer to shift from being open with God to being some sort of religious game.

My religious pretensions do not fool God. They only get in the way of my receiving what God is offering. God is continually reaching out to embrace us humans, but we block God's embrace by hiding behind a phony image of ourselves. Rather than being humbly open *with* God and open *to* God, we drift into trying to impress and manipulate God. God knows the difference between the persons we pretend to be and the persons we really are; however, we do not always recognize the difference.

By hanging on to pretensions I am the one who is fooled, not God. I am the real loser because when I am unwilling to be open and honest with God, my phoniness gets in the way of the healing, hope, and empowerment God has to offer. How can I be open to receive what God offers me in my anger if I am busy denying I am angry? How can I be open to receive what God offers me in my envy if I pretend I have no envy? How can I be open to receive what God offers to deal with my neediness if I deny I need anything? I cannot be open *to* what God has to offer, if I am not open *with* God about my living.

Hypocrisy, playing games, not being open with God, does not limit what God knows. My pretending before God that I love my enemy and forgive my foes does not blind God to my hate and desire for revenge. God does not need my confession in order to know who I am, what I have done, what I really desire, and what I really fear. But I need to confess because I need to stop pretending in order to be open to what God is offering. My hypocrisy and playing religious games do not fool God. They only demonstrate my foolishness as I continue pretending in front of a mirror or performing in front of an audience. When I am not open *with* God, I am unable to be open *to* God and unable to receive what God is offering. Then, all I can receive are the quickly evaporating rewards that come relative to my skill in playing religious games.

Jesus taught his disciples that the humility of simple and profound honesty is what God desires in our praying. Prayer is an act of intimacy with God—not a religious trick to get God to do what we want or a performance we do for recognition from others. Our prayers are not graded as if praying were some sort of heavenly speech test. There are no extra points for eloquence with human words. Jesus taught all who would listen that what God wants from us is a genuine relationship of faith (profound trust), not information or a sales pitch. God already knows more about us than we know about ourselves—including what we really desire. Besides, God sees through flowery speech. What God really wants is humble, honest intimacy.

"And when you pray, you must not be like the hypocrites; for they love to stand and pray in the synagogues and at the street corners, that they may be seen by others. Truly, I say to you, they have recieved their reward. But when you pray, go into your room and shut the door and pray to your Father who is in secret; and your Father who sees in secret will reward you.

"And in praying do not heap up empty phrases as the Gentiles do; for they think that they will be heard for their many words. Do not be like them, for your Father knows what you need before you ask Him" (Matt 6:7–8).

For Meditation and Conversation

1. What does prayer that is open *with* God look like?

2. What does prayer that is open *to* God look like?

3. For what are you grateful?

4. What do you really want?

5. What is worrying you, frightening you?

6. Aware of these realities, what is your prayer, that is, in what ways are you open with and open to God regarding these realities in your life?

22

Pray Then Like This: "Our Father . . ."

MATTHEW 6:9

Jesus knew the question in the minds of his disciples: "How shall we pray?" This question has to do with more than the correct choice of words or the correct form or style of speech to be be employed in praying.

Prayer is first of all a question of honesty, of being completely open with God. How can we humans lay down the heavy load of masks we carry? We have one for every occasion: masks we have been given and taught to wear, masks we use to obtain what we want and avoid what we fear. How can we push aside the camouflage that our true self hides under, or behind? How can we be open with God, neither pretending a goodness beyond us nor engaging in the confession of trivial sins while avoiding recognition of the deeper cancer of sin in our soul? How can we heave an honest sigh and simply be who we are before our Creator? How can we be open *with* God?

That is part of the question. The other part is how can we be open *to* God. How do we listen to that which is beyond all the noise of our circumstance, listen through all the talking that goes on inside our heads, listen beyond all the distractions that call for our attention and all the temptations that call for our affection? How can we discern God's will for our daily living?

How can we be open *with* God and *to* God? How shall we pray?

"Pray then like this," Jesus said. "Our Father . . ."

In demonstrating the way to pray, Jesus was not merely giving his disciples magic words to say. He was showing them how to approach God. He told the disciples to pray to God in the way a child approaches a loving father. (Remember, the Aramaic word Jesus used was closer to the English word *Daddy* than *Father.*) In calling God "Father," the disciples would not merely be saying that they believed God exists, any more than a little girl saying "Daddy" is merely declaring she believes that her father exists. Jesus was teaching those who would listen to approach God in faith, trusting the love of God the way little children come to their loving fathers or mothers.

After all, the One Jesus taught the disciples to call Father is like an ideal parent—not one of those parents who abuse through neglect or lust or fear or plain old meanness. God is not the father who leaves scars both seen and hidden. God is not the father who lives out of old pain or secret guilt and leaves his children the legacy of living with regrets and resentments. To call God Father is not to speak of an ordinary parent. God is like the ideal parent, who loves without clinging or controlling, who loves with tenderness beyond the sentimental, who loves with toughness that will not quit, a tough love strong enough to allow the consequences to happen so that we might convert from the way we are to the way God meant us to be. All this and more is what Jesus was teaching when he told the disciples to pray addressing God as their Father.

It is also important to notice that this prayer Jesus taught does not begin, "*My* Father" but rather "*Our* Father." When we say God is *our* Father, we are saying more than that God cannot be exclusively claimed by me or by you or by anyone. We are not only declaring that God is the God of all people; we are also saying that all humans are our brothers and sisters. All of us humans have the same status: children of God. God is *our* Father.

There is no one-upmanship in the family of God. Powerless and powerful, rich and poor, beautiful and ugly, talented and untalented, responsible and irresponsible, polite and crude, intelligent and unintelligent, deformed and normal, good and bad—all and each are loved by God. All and each are God's children. When we truly pray "Our Father," we can no longer justify standing apart from one another, isolating "them" from "us." We are brothers and sisters. We belong to the same family.

The demonstration prayer declared: "Our Father who is in heaven . . ." As I stated in a previous chapter, heaven is not a place located somewhere just beyond the sun and stars of our galaxy, or just beyond all the galaxies in the universe. God is not confined by space and time. Heaven is not a place to which we finally escape—a never-ending paradise for those who successfully retire from a career as human being. Heaven is not a place in the usual way we speak of place. Heaven is a reality of holy mystery.

God is in heaven, not in our concepts of heaven. God is in heaven, and heaven is wherever God reigns in this life and in the life to come. As the poet who wrote Ps 139 made clear, there is no getting away from God. God is wherever the divine "what ought to be" is in the process of overcoming the "unholy mess of what is." God is wherever love hangs on and is unwilling to give way to all the fears that drain love from the hearts of God's children. God is wherever hope in that which is eternal heals despair over that which is temporal. God is wherever good lives in the midst of evil. God is wherever divine justice and mercy mingle together in unity. Heaven is where God truly reigns, where God's will is done.

God is in life, in death, in life beyond death. Our human concepts of time and space are inadequate for comprehending the full mystery of the reality of God's presence in life, and in life beyond death. It is in embracing this mystery that we begin to pray, and we begin our prayer saying, "Our Father who art in heaven."

We are to say it, not merely recite it like some schoolchild seeking the teacher's approval. We are to say it, really say it, like children imitating the way God talked when God said, "Let there be light" and then light really happened. It all begins when, like children who are created in the image of God, we say to God, "Our Father who art in heaven" and really mean it—mean it so much that saying it and living it are one and the same. When we declare that God is our Father and allow the image of God within us to shape our living, our saying "Our Father" is not merely reciting words, but rather a profound affirmation of the way life is.

There is more. God is not only our Father, God is holy. God is neither an indulgent daddy nor an abusive father. God is the Ineffable Reality, the maker and sustainer of all that is, who, for reasons beyond common sense, has chosen to love us the way an ideal parent loves. When we begin to comprehend the truth these flimsy words point toward, we are filled with awe and an awareness of the specialness of God that we call "holy." "Hallowed be thy name," Jesus taught his disciples to pray—or in other words, "Holy is who you are."

When we are able to embrace the truth that God is both Father and holy, this awareness impacts the way we live. We live in joyful awe and faithfulness that truly glorifies God. Or to say that more poetically, our living causes God to smile. Giving glory to God, glorifying God, honoring who God is, is not accomplished in special religious talk and singing; it is accomplished in living shaped by an awareness of God being both Father and holy. Then, our talk and singing are more than merely talk and singing, and our praying "Our Father who art in heaven, hallowed be thy name" is something more than stating a theological opinion we have been taught to repeat.

"Pray then like this: 'Our Father who art in heaven, Hallowed be thy name'" (Matt 6:9).

For Meditation and Conversation

1. What do you discern to be the implications of prayer that is completely open with and open to God?

2. Meditate on and then have conversation about what we are praying when, with faithful integrity, we pray:

"Our Father"

"who art in heaven"

"hallowed be thy name."

23

"Thy Kingdom Come; Thy Will Be Done"

MATTHEW 6:10

IT TAKES NO PROFOUND theologian to proclaim, "Life is not the way God intends it to be." All it takes is a bit of pain and a dash of injustice, stirred into dissolving hope and flavored with heartache and grief. "Thy kingdom come" can easily become the pathetic plea of a disillusioned dreamer longing for the bad guys, at long last, to get what they really deserve in some sort of last day of damning judgment, while the good guys—always us—finally get our long overdue reward, namely, all the honors and delights we have been longing for. "Thy kingdom come; Thy will be done" is an easy prayer to pray as long as we believe that God is on our side and that the will of God is consistent with all of our desires.

But what about other times? What about those times when, in our ignorance or sin or both, our desires conflict with God's will? In such times, we are unable to recognize God's kingdom in front of our noses and unable to believe that "that" (whatever "that" is) could possibly be God's will. And what about those times when we know what we ought to do but we do not want to do it? In those situations, our honest prayer is more likely to be another prayer (or rather part of a prayer) we learned from Jesus: "Let this cup pass from me" (Matt 16:39; Mark 14:36; Luke 22:42).

When Jesus taught the disciples, and all who would listen, to pray, "Thy kingdom come," he was talking about sincerely longing for God to reign in our lives and all of life. All too often this is not what we really want. I suppose Jesus knew this about us, and that is why he went on to underscore what he was instructing us to desire from God: "Thy will be done."

Most of the time, when I utter this prayer, what I really want is God's reign to fulfill my longings and for God's will to be the same as mine. That is when I use my reasoning skills to convince myself that what God really wants is what I want. I twist the petition "Thy kingdom come; Thy will be done" into a self-serving prayer that aligns God's desires with mine.

But God is beyond human manipulation. We cannot control God. To realize that God is both holy *and* wholly other is to be confronted with the difference between God and us. God is not merely a superhuman being subject to the same kinds of manipulation that we humans are. For those of us who have understandably embraced the fantasy of being able to get God to do our bidding, this can be a most disturbing and humbling realization.

To pray as Jesus taught the disciples to pray—"Thy kingdom come; Thy will be done"—is to utter a prayer of surrender. To pray sincerely, "Thy kingdom come; Thy will be done on earth" is to ask for change, for conversion. This prayer, when it is sincerely prayed, is the honest longing for God to reign in all of life, in all lives, beginning with our own. This prayer is not about God making our lives the way we want them to be; it is all about God making our lives as God intends them to be.

The difference between reciting these words as a religious exercise and offering them as prayer is the difference between empty talk and earnest effort. "Thy kingdom come; Thy will be done" is an authentic prayer when our words are accompanied by our striving to let go of self-centeredness and selfishness. Jesus was teaching the disciples and all who would listen that the genuineness of our prayer is measured by our willingness to trust God with our lives, with all we call "ours," with all that is.

The genuineness of our prayer is reflected in the way we live, and when we live "Thy will be done on earth as it is in heaven," we move beyond merely asking God to "fix it." When our prayer is genuine, we actually become involved in struggling to discern and do God's will on earth as it is done where God reigns. Our living makes our saying the words of prayer something other than sounds babbled into space. It is when the prayer from our lips is consistent with the living of our lives that saying this bit of memorized Scripture is transformed into praying. Until we strive to live it, we have not yet begun to pray it because authentic prayer involves being completely honest with God.

The prayer Jesus prayed into life and lived into prayer, the prayer he taught his disciples to imitate in word and deed, is not a cry of desperation. It was and is a hymn of confident commitment. It is not a plea of pain-filled longing and despair making a desperate grab at hope. It is a confident call for God, who has the game already won, to speed us along in living God's will so that the homecoming victory dance can begin.

"Thy kingdom come. Thy will be done, on earth as it is in heaven" (Matt 6:10).

For Meditation and Conversation

Meditate on what Jesus was teaching us in this part of the prayer, and then discuss:

"Thy kingdom come."
"Thy will be done, on earth as it is in heaven."

24

"Give Us This Day Our Daily Bread"

MATTHEW 6:11

WHEN JESUS SAID, "PRAY like this," he not only demonstrated how to pray; at a deeper level, he was giving his disciples yet another lesson in how to live. When he prayed, "Give us this day our daily bread," it was a clear demonstration of being aware of our dependence on God.

We talk about "earning our daily bread." There is obvious truth in the statement. We (or someone working on our behalf) invest labor for daily bread—not merely for food, but for all the basic necessities. This is the way the world is. Someone has to break the ground, cultivate the field, plant the seed, tend the crop, harvest the grain, turn it into flour, and do the kitchen work of turning flour into bread. Houses do not just appear out of the blue, nor does clothing. Someone's labor is required to pay the bills.

Certainly, Jesus was aware of this bit of reality. Nevertheless, the prayer Jesus taught his disciples does not say, "Help us earn our daily bread"; it says, "Give us this day our daily bread." What was he trying to teach his disciples?

Jesus understood that life is a gift. In his teaching us to pray, "Give us this day our daily bread," he was demonstrating that although it is true that we must work, we also need to understand that everything we have is a gift. Jesus was teaching all who would listen not to be confused by the amount of labor we must do to stay alive. Just as a farmer with profound insight and faith knows that apart from the mystery of God's creative grace, no crop will grow, there is something more involved in our receiving our daily bread than our labor alone.

Jesus was not saying, "What you do does not matter." He was saying that even the ability to earn our daily bread is a gift from God. He was saying, in effect, "Do not be misled by all you have and by all you have accomplished. Examine your lives carefully and profoundly and you will discover that all your abilities and opportunities are, finally and ultimately, gifts." Jesus wanted all who would listen to realize that even when they had exerted great effort, working long hours to achieve whatever they had achieved, even then, if they viewed life the way that Jesus did, they would realize that all they were and all they had was ultimately a gift of God's grace.

This is why, when we pray, "Give us this day our daily bread," we are talking like children who gratefully acknowledge that everything they have is a gift. "Give us this day our daily bread" is not to be spoken as if we are royalty demanding service from our servant. Nor is it appropriate for us to speak as customers who have paid their bills and now demand what is rightfully theirs. Nor are we to beg, with hands outstretched and eyes downcast, looking at the dirt, like someone with no sense of self-worth.

We are to pray to God in the way that a confident child comes to the ideal, loving Parent—our Father. We are to come as a child who knows his or her dependence but who comes confidently trusting this parent and this parent's love. With the confidence of children who know they are truly loved, we ask for our daily bread—neither demanding nor begging. Jesus was teaching us to ask as a child of God, reaching out, confidently trusting the grace of God.

In praying for our daily bread, Jesus was aware that we are asking for more than the bread made of wheat that keeps our bodies going. He understood that we also need the kind of food that keeps our souls alive, and this soul food is obviously more than bread made with flour. It is more than all the material goods we need in order to survive physically. The kind of bread that is soul food is everything necessary for not merely staying alive but for being *alive*! It is the kind of bread that is made of more than flour. It is the bread of the Gospel. We are to feed on the good news of God's grace. This is the bread that faithful people sing about: "Bread of heaven, bread of heaven, feed me till I want no more."[1]

---

1. "Guide Me, O Thou Great Jehovah"; words by William Williams.

The goal of life is more than mere physical well-being. Thus, the prayer "Give us this day our daily bread" is not only our prayer for physical survival, but it is also our prayer for all that we need to be fully alive as God intends us to be. Jesus was acutely aware that all that brings vitality into our living is a gift of grace—a gift not to be received just once in a lifetime but daily.

For example, our sense of worth and purpose is, at the deepest level, a gift. From a variety of sources, we discover who we are and who we are meant to be. This discovery is not merely a once-in-a-lifetime gift. It is a gift to be affirmed and confirmed day after day after day. Discovering what gives us a sense of purpose and joy is a great and wonderful gift, and it is a gift we need to receive again and again.

Jesus was teaching his disciples to live in the awareness of their dependence on God, who cares for them like the ideal Parent, and to ask for what they need, one day at a time. "Give us this day our daily bread."

God gives us life one day at a time; thus, all we need is what we need to live our lives one day at a time. It is tempting to ask for more—especially when we have doubts about the future. Pain and the fear of pain (either physical or emotional) tempt us to try to control the future in order to make all our tomorrows safe and secure. But all the insurance, investments, and planning we can do will not ensure our security. No one controls tommorow. The outlook on life of US citizens on September 10, 2001, was not what it was on September 12, 2001. It is one thing, having harvested the crop, to store up what we need to make it until the next harvest; it is something else to try to live more than one day at a time. To live our lives trying to control all our tomorrows while taking care of our responsibilities today is to try to handle more than we were created to handle. Jesus was demonstrating the way to live when he gave the disciples this demonstration of prayer. One day at a time is more than enough for us to handle faithfully.

Jesus was clearly aware of what anyone knows when he or she stops to think. To make tomorrow safe and secure is finally beyond what we humans are able to achieve, because the possibilities in tomorrow are beyond our knowing and way beyond our controlling. Even living only one day at a time, we cannot be certain of what is truly good for us. What looked like a wise choice yesterday can look like a stupid decision tomorrow, and vice versa. Even less can we be certain that we know what will be good for others tomorrow. Because all any of us ever really have is now (this day), Jesus taught us to pray as children who trust their ideal, loving Parent, asking only for the bread to keep their bodies going, and for the Bread of Life to keep their souls alive one day at a time.

It is also important to notice that Jesus did not teach his disciples to pray, "Give me" but rather "Give us." Our asking is not to be centered on "me" and "mine" but on "us" and "our." Our asking is like that of a child asking on behalf of the whole family—the whole human family. Thus, our asking "Give us this day our daily bread" is far from selfishness. It is an act of love that reaches far beyond the concerns for me and mine.

Jesus was teaching his disciples confidently to trust God the way a child trusts an ideal parent. Aware of their profound dependence on God, and aware of the need of all people for nourishment of body and soul, they learned from Jesus to pray.

"Give us this day our daily bread" (Matt 6:11).

For Meditation and Conversation

Meditate on this petition by focusing on the individual parts of the prayer, and then discuss:

> "*Give* us this day our daily bread."
> "Give *us* this day our daily bread."
> "Give us *this day* our daily bread."
> "Give us this day *our daily bread.*"

25

"Forgive Us . . . as We Have Forgiven"

MATTHEW 6:12

I N THIS PRAYER, AS well as in Jesus' comments that immediately follow it and in deeds throughout his ministry, Jesus taught the disciples that accepting forgiveness and forgiving others are inseparable. Both receiving forgiveness and giving forgiveness are essential for living as God intends us to live.

A man nearing fifty years of age entered my study; his anger was clearly visible. Expletives of rage freely punctuated the story he told about being treated unjustly when his father died. It was not until he was several minutes into his story that I discovered that the injustice he was talking about had happened when he was twenty years old. He was imprisoned in his decades of rage toward the people he was convinced had ruined his life. His inability to forgive and move on had increased his torture in the dark dungeon of self-pity and hatred to which he had confined himself. His bondage to past injustice had crippled his ability to take advantage of other opportunities. Each of these failures increased his self-contempt, which intensified the anger and resentment he felt about what had happened almost thirty years before.

Failure to forgive can cripple our ability to move on and live creatively. When Jesus said, "Pray then like this: 'Forgive us . . . as we have forgiven,'" he was not saying, "God will not forgive us unless we forgive others," as though we controlled God. Jesus knew that our refusing to forgive distorts our living so that we end up in misery, similar to the angry man who came to visit me. Not only had he suffered the consequences of failing to forgive and move on, his misery had splashed on everyone he had dealt with across the years. Unwilling to forgive, and enslaved by his anger, self-pity, and resentment, his living was distorted, and that caused distortion in all his relationships. Jesus knew that for us to be able to live as God intends, forgiveness is essential.

So what is forgiveness?

Forgiveness is not some sort of delete button that erases from our memory the harm that was done to us. Forgiveness is not some form of holy amnesia. If it were, we would gain no wisdom from our pain. Forgiveness sets us free to learn from the past without being in bondage to it.

Forgiveness does not give someone a "do-over." Life is not like making a movie in which the actors do take after take until they get it right. In real life, what has happened, has happened. Forgiveness does not undo the pain that was caused or the damage that was done. Forgiveness is what prevents the pain we experienced and the damage that was done in the past from controlling our living today—even though what was done has limited or altered the options we now have.

Sometimes we confuse forgiveness with reconciliation; and when we do, we embrace the illusion that merely forgiving someone will bring healing to the relationship. This confusion often leads to disappointment and sometimes additional bitterness. While forgiveness makes reconciliation a possibility, it takes more than forgiveness for a relationship to be healed.

What forgiveness does is to allow the one who does the forgiving to move on without being enslaved by the wrong that was done. Our forgiving sets us free from the resentments and old angers that can control and distort our living. When we forgive, we are no longer in bondage to the wrong that was done to us; and therefore it is possible for us to be open to the possibility of reconciliation. Our forgiveness does not make reconciliation happen, but it opens the door.

For example, if I have done you harm, I am not likely to apologize (what the church calls "confession of sin") or change my behavior (what the church calls "repentance") as long as I sense you are unwilling to forgive me. Your forgiving me does not insure that I will apologize and change; but if you are unforgiving, I am not likely to admit the wrong I have done, and I am less likely to change. Without your forgiveness, the door to reconciliation remains closed. Forgiveness is not the same thing as reconciliation, but for reconciliation to happen, forgiveness is one of the essential ingredients.

Whether we are aware of it or not, it is God's grace, especially God's merciful love at work in our lives, that enables us to forgive. Jesus was aware that the more we allow the grace of God to shape our living, the more we are in harmony with God; and the more we are in harmony with God, the more willing we are to forgive others. It is being in harmony with God that creates the kind of wholeness of soul that is needed in order to forgive as Jesus forgave.

How to live in harmony with God, how to receive this wholeness of soul, lies at the heart of Jesus' teaching. From what little we know about the disciples, it is evident they were eager to learn. Why else would they have made the sacrifices they made in order to be his students (disciples), following him around the country in order to participate in his traveling seminar? While it is clear from even a casual reading of the four Gospels that the disciples often misunderstood, and at times failed, they were open to learning.

They were learning that God is like parents who so love their child that they see potential in the child that the neighbors are unable to see or imagine. Jesus' treatment of those who were social outcasts demonstrated the kind of love that sees potential in persons whom other people have written off as lost causes. Jesus saw the potential God sees and was more concerned about what could be than about what had been. When we forgive, we experience both the gift of being set free from bondage to old hurts and the gift of trusting in the potential for good that is present.

Our being forgiven does not eliminate or undo the consequences that our past behavior set in motion. But when we accept forgiveness, even as we suffer through the consequences of the sinful choices that we made, God's grace makes us alert to the positive possibilities in the midst of our mess.

Neither forgiving nor accepting forgiveness can deny or undo the past. They set us free from being imprisoned in the past because forgiveness focuses on the positive potential in the present and the future. This focus liberates us from living enslaved by what we did or what others did in days gone by.

In God's forgiveness of us, God sees the mess we have made, but God also sees more than the mess. God sees what and who we can yet be. God sees the possibility of new beginnings in the midst of our mess; God sees the possibility of our conversion from the way we are to the way God intends us to be. God's vision of the positive possibilities yet before us and God's longing for us to fulfill the potential God sees is the way God's merciful love is expressed through forgiveness.

So it is in our forgiving others. When we forgive, we are setting ourselves free from remaining in bondage to the aftermath of the wrong that was done. But more than that, when our forgiveness is coupled with mercy, we are more concerned about the positive potential in the future than the mess that is in the past; after all, the past is past and cannot be undone. Only the present and future are open to new possibility, but that new possibility exists only if we allow the past to be past.

As I mentioned earlier, having new possiblity does not exempt anyone from the consequences of their past, but it does acknowledge and allow for new and posititive possiblities in the present and future. So forgiveness of others includes trusting that there are positive possibilities in the one (or ones) we are forgiving, just as God's merciful forgiveness of us focuses on the positive possibilities available in our relationship with God. In my personal experience, my ability to forgive is directly related to my being aware of my being forgiven and trusting that I can live into the positive potential God sees in my future.

Those who know themselves to be truly forgiven are those who are the most forgiving. Conversely, those who are insensitive to their own need for forgiveness not only tend to be insensitive to the forgiveness God is offering but also tend to be unforgiving of others.

Jesus saw that the primary sign or symptom of our having accepted God's forgiveness is our willingness to forgive others. Forgiving and being forgiven are inseparable. This is what Jesus was teaching when he said:

"*And forgive us our debts* [trespasses, sins], *as we also have forgiven our debtors* [those who have trespassed against us, sinned against us]." (Matt 6:12).

For Meditation and Conversation

1. What is forgiveness and what is it not?

2. What is the wisdom of Jesus tying our request to be forgiven to our willingness to forgive others?

3. To what extent does your awareness of having been forgiven affect your willingness and ability to forgive?

26

"Lead Us Not into Temptation, but Deliver Us from Evil"

MATTHEW 6:13A

THE TACTIC THAT ENABLES or allows evil to control our living is seldom a frontal attack, but rather the tactic of infiltration. That which distorts and destroys life (what the Bible calls "evil") usually takes over our lives from inside us. Evil uses our desires, which are not in and of themselves evil, to lure us into evil. For example, the desire for comfort, power, security, and wealth lured people in the colonial states to rationalize slavery. The result is that we in the United States are still dealing with the myriad consequences of the actions of our ancestors—Africans selling other Africans to the owners of slave ships, who had them auctioned by professional auctioneers to be purchased by planters, all done for the sake of gaining wealth. Today, the consequences of slavery prove the truth of what was declared in Gen 20:5—that the iniquity of the parents impacts the children of the third and fourth generations.

"Lead us not into temptation, but deliver us from evil," Jesus taught his disciples to pray.

I would be greatly surprised if any of those responsible for the scandal and financial collapse of Enron, or the financial crisis that has driven the United States into incomprehensible debt, would ever have considered breaking into someone's home to steal money. Yet, from all the news reports, it is obvious that executives of corporations and financial institutions were so tempted by the lure of wealth that they willingly participated in unethical, if not criminal, schemes that brought financial harm to millions of individuals and families. Many of us contributed to the mess through our purchase of more than we could realistically afford.

"Lead us not into temptation, but deliver us from evil," Jesus taught all who would listen to pray.

We are subject to many temptations. Sometimes the tempations we experience make us so gullible that others take advantage of us. Other times our desires tempt us to take advantage of others—sometimes for profit, sometimes for prestige, sometimes for personal pleasure.

The more self-centered we become, the more likely we are to view other people not as persons of worth but as pawns to be manipulated to help us get what we want. When self-centered goals shape our living, we easily develop a mind-set that not only makes us vulnerable to being used by others but also makes us insensitive to the harm we are doing to others, and insensitive to the long-term consequences for ourselves as well as for those who follow us.

"Lead us not into temptation," Jesus taught his disciples to pray.

Jesus knew about temptation firsthand (Matt 4:1–11 and Luke 4:1–13). He was aware that we are easily seduced by the temptation to forget others, to ignore God, and to focus only on what serves us in the present moment. When we do, there is "hell to pay," as Grandpa would have said. When we give in to temptations, it is only a matter of time until the consequences cause pain and problems for others, for ourselves, and all too often, even for our children, grandchildren, and great-grandchildren.

This truth of the long-range consequences that sin lets loose has been painfully demonstrated in our country's continuing to struggle with the ongoing consequences of the sin of slavery. Slavery is just one example of the kinds of complex, destructive forces and hurtful consequences that are summed up in the Bible by the word *evil*.

Evil is the reality at work in persons and systems that abuse and destructively manipulate other individuals or other groups. Evil is the complex of subtle pressures that seduce us to participate in or at least not object to behaviors that are unjust, negative, destructive, oppressive, and cruel. Evil is what urges us to respond to greed with greed, hate with hate, suspicion with suspicion, and hurt with hurt. Evil is a subtle, destructive reality tempting us to believe that it is the way smart people live.

This destructive reality that distorts life outside ourselves finds its way inside us, distorting the way we live, seducing us to participate in evil. Within us, voices tempt us away from our best selves. Our old wounds can lure us to be resentful and seek revenge. Remembered pain tempts us toward self-pity—and tempts us to rationalize and excuse our destructive behavior and the pain we inflict on others. There are within us voices conjuring visions of bad things that might happen and freezing out compassion with fear. There are within us voices seductively describing illusions with such artistry that we mistake fantasy for reality. There are within us voices declaring with such eloquence that what we have is ours, that we no longer see our lives as gifts. There are within us voices calling into question the rights of others to their blessings, justifying our envy and motivating our schemes to take from them what is theirs. There are within us voices whispering about our lack of worth and eloquently listing our faults and failures while denying any significant value in our gifts. There are within us voices luring us into the fog where the quicksand of depression and despair suck us under. From the darkest corners of the basement of our subconscious, voices send us twisted messages that trigger in us such fear that we seek relief in the angers of prejudice, blaming scapegoats for the mess we are in.

Jesus knew about the destructive realities that push on us from the outside and the destructive voices that seduce us from deep within ourselves. He knew about temptation and evil. So he taught any who would listen to pray, "Lead us not into temptation, but deliver us from evil."

He knew that alone we are no match for those damning realities and their voices within us. Our intellectual insight is too easily seduced by rationalizations that justify our use, misuse, and abuse of others. Our willpower has only the power for a short-term sprint, and we are in a lifelong marathon. Our basic goodness is so flawed with self-serving, and so easily abandoned, that we pretend our unholy rage is "righteous anger." Alone we are no match for all that would distort and destroy our lives and seduce us (at times even wearing the camouflage of religious devotion) into spreading distortion and destruction. Left to ourselves, we do not have the strength to resist evil.

How are we to cope? Where is hope? Clues can be found in the story of Jesus struggling with temptation (Matt 4:1–11 and Luke 4:1–13). When he was tempted to use his gifts and abilities for self-centered purposes, Jesus was able to say no because he kept his focus on a greater good. He did not merely use human willpower to "just say no." He was able to say no because of what he was saying yes to. He resisted temptation because he kept his focus on a greater good—God and God's will.

Jesus knew that the way to fight evil is to keep our focus on the good while striving to attain the good. In dealing with evil, we are tempted to forget the good and only fight that which is evil—which curiously results in our becoming involved in some other form of evil. One can see this dynamic at work in all wars, including the "War on Terror." In fighting what is obviously evil, it is easy to forget the good that is essential and to drift toward behavior that is subtly similar to the evil we are fighting. Because it is easy to be unaware of drifting away from the greater good in life, Jesus dealt with evil and his temptations by intentionally and explicitly keeping his focus on the greater good of serving God. It is by keeping our focus on what is good and especially on the greatest good that we are able to reject the temptation to evil.

Jesus identified the focus we need. "Deliver us from evil, for thine is the kingdom, the power and the glory forever." It is in keeping our focus on the greater good (the greatest good)—God—that God is able to deliver us from evil. When we forget the One to whom the power and glory really belong, we are easily seduced by temptation and become pawns of evil.

Our hope is in God—God as revealed in and through Jesus. Only as we seek God and long for what is good are we able to allow the grace of God to lead us away from temptations and the trials they bring. Our only hope is focusing on God and God-defined goodness—the kind of goodness we can see in Christ. By focusing on the goodness revealed by God in Christ and trusting God's love made known in Jesus, we are open to God's guidance, have access to resources of grace, and are able to pursue the good.

It is in pursuing what is good that God enables us to resist what is evil. But we need the help of God to do that. Our willpower alone is not strong enough. We need God's help. Jesus knew this, and so he taught all who would listen to pray:

"And lead us not into temptation, but deliver us from evil" (Matt 1:13a).

For Meditation and Conversation

1. What are the temptations outside yourself that are most seductive?

2. What are the temptations from within that are the most alluring?

3. What leads us into temptation?

4. What is your understanding of "evil" and deliverance from it?

27

"For Thine Is the Kingdom and the Power and the Glory Forever. Amen."

MATTHEW 6:13B

O N A HILLSIDE BY the Sea of Gaililee, Jesus taught his disciples that chasing the illusion that we control life is not only a waste of time but also a distortion of who we are meant to be. God is our Creator; we are the sheep of his pasture (Ps 95:7). Any claims to the contrary are illusions out of touch with God, the Ultimate Reality. "Thine is the kingdom, the power and the glory," Jesus taught his disciples. He taught them to live focused on the truth that the only God is the One he called Father—not ourselves or something else.

He taught them to pray "*Thine* is the kingdom" because he knew that we humans so easily forget that God is finally in charge. In our foolish attempts to create our own little kingdoms, we waste our limited time and energy. There is only one kingdom that matters—God's kingdom. As I stated earlier, God's kingdom is where God reigns, and God's reigning is what "kingdom" language is all about. The issue addressed in this part of the prayer has to do with who really is boss. Who really owns it all? To whom is all reality finally accountable? Ultimately, all belongs to God: "*Thine* is the kingdom."

Nevertheless, we dream of being in charge, of having the power to control our destiny. "If only I can get that job, get that promotion, make that deal, obtain that position, then I will have it made." We dream of having power to control life so that life will be what we want it to be for ourselves and those we love. In pursuit of that dream, we wear ourselves out trying to obtain wealth, believing that wealth will give us the power to be in control. Others of us exhaust ourselves trying to gain popularity so that through the power of being liked we can prove our importance. I think this is why so many people seem to have a cult-like devotion to celebrities, devouring magazine articles about them and watching TV shows that feature their latest exploits. It is the illusion that these people temporarily in the spolight, by being well known and popular, have achieved what we desire. Or we pursue knowledge and skills, believing that possession of knowledge and skills will make our lives worth living. Forgetting who we are and whose we are, we use up our limited time and energy in the needless pursuit of being in charge of our lives. Jesus was teaching all who would listen to remember that only God is truly in charge: "*Thine* is the the kingdom and the power."

As much as we may want power, we also want glory. However, Jesus taught us that the glory also belongs to God. Yet we want the recognition, the appreciation, the applause, the glory. "Look what I did," we say. Of course, sometimes we do something of worth, and people applaud or reward us with some sort of pay. Jesus was aware that a laborer is worthy of his wages (Luke 10:7). It is appropriate to derive satisfaction and joy from the fruits of our labor. Without arrogance, we are to delight in what our head and hands can produce, and like a small child at show-and-tell, we say, "Look what I did." We are to delight in our labor and give God the glory for providing the gifts involved.

It is vital that we stay in touch with reality, remembering that what we accomplish is like the science project of a child on which the parent did a major part of the work. It is appropriate for children to be proud of their contribution to the project. But it is a lie for children to talk and act as if they did it all. When we ignore what God has done and pretend that we did it all by ourselves, our claim of "Look what I did" is such a half-truth that it borders on blasphemy. The glory really belongs to God. When we pretend otherwise, we live a lie, like a child lying to the teacher by denying how much the parent did on the science project.

The kingdom and the power and the glory have always belonged to God, and they always will. This is the way it has always been. This is the way it will always be. Our saying "Amen" to all that is in this prayer is a way of affirming and declaring, "That's the truth."

"For Thine is the kingdom and the power and the glory, forever. Amen" (Matt 6:13b).

For Meditation and Conversation

What are the implications for daily living that you discern in each part of this prayerful declaration and affirmation:

"For thine is the kingdom"
"and the power"
"and the glory"
"forever."
"Amen."

28

The Forgiven Are to Forgive

"LET ME SAY THIS one more time . . ." we say in our efforts to teach. Somewhere I read that new information must be heard seven times before it is grasped. I do not know about the number of repetitions it takes, but I do know that repetition is vital to learning. Also, repeating what we have said is one way that we emphasize the importance of what we are trying to communicate. It is a technique to ensure that what we are saying will not be overlooked.

Jesus said it before; now he says it again to be sure that we get the message. Forgiving others is not merely important, it is essential. Forgiving others is the primary sign, the key indicator, of who really has accepted the gift of grace, of who really has accepted salvation. The point is so important that Jesus does not want to risk his disciples' missing it. Unless we embrace our having been forgiven and are willing to forgive others, our works of justice will be distorted by our guilt or by our self-righteousness, and our works of mercy will be anemic or absent.

To refuse to forgive while claiming forgiveness is the height of illusion and the depth of self-deception. Claiming that we are forgiven, yet being unwilling to forgive, is spiritual suicide because when we are unwilling to forgive, anger, resentment, and the desire to get even destroy the health in our souls in the way that cancer devours healthy tissue. When we are soul-sick with anger and resentment, we will even use our religion to bless our lust for revenge and to justify our refusal to forgive.

Convinced we are in the right, we are insensitive to our hypocrisy and unaware of spiritually shooting ourselves in the foot. We can be so caught up in self-righteousness that vitality is drained from our souls until we are spiritually dead without even being aware of it. And so we persist in our self-condemning damnation of others, unaware that we are victims of our self-righteous desires and efforts to get even and make "them" pay.

Some people may still misunderstand and ask, but doesn't what you are saying undermine grace? You seem to be declaring that we are saved by our own works, including the work of forgiving others. What about being saved by grace through faith and not because works, lest we should boast? (Eph 2:8–9)

Forgiving others is not what brings us forgiveness or salvation. Forgiving others is our reflecting the grace that shines on us and through us. Our forgiving others is a byproduct of the grace we have received. Our failure to forgive is a symptom of our failure to embrace the forgiveness that has been given us.

The only way God's grace can be truly ours is like water flowing through a garden hose. To claim forgiveness for ourselves but to be unwilling to give it to others is to have such a kink in our souls that God's grace and forgiveness fail to flow through us to others. When we are like a garden hose with kinks in it, we stop grace from flowing into and through our lives. The water is not cut off, it simply cannot flow because of the kinks in our living. When grace is unable to flow into us because we are unwilling to allow it to flow through us, we are as useless to God as a garden hose through which water is unable to flow, and we are ready for the garbage dump.

When we refuse to forgive, we reveal the absence of grace in our lives. The First Letter of John puts it this way: "We love because he [God] first loved us. If anyone says, 'I love God,' and hates his brother, he is a liar; for he who does not love his brother whom he has seen, cannot love God whom he has not seen" (4:19–20).[1]

The meaning of these verses becomes more clear when we remember that the Greek word for love used in this passage is *agape*, which refers less to feelings and emotions than to ethics and the decision to act on behalf of what is good for others. The writer of First John was saying if we cannot give of ourselves for the good of our neighbor, then we are kid-

---

1. See chapter 9 of this book dealing with Matthew 5:8.

ding ourselves if we think that we have a good relationship with God. It is also wise to remember that earlier Jesus said the command to love our neighbor includes even those we call our enemies.[2]

The primary sign or symptom of our having received and accepted God's grace is in the way it flows through us to others.

"For if you forgive men [others] *their trespasses, your heavenly Father also will forgive you; but if you do not forgive men* [others] *their trespasses, neither will your Father forgive your trespasses"* (Matt 6:14–15).

For Meditation and Conversation

1. Why do you think Jesus emphasized forgiveness? Why is it important for our daily living?

2. Describe your perception of how your forgiving others is linked to or is a by-product of your being forgiven.

---

2. See chapter 19 dealing with Matthew 5:43–48.

29

Phony Faithfulness

MATTHEW 6:16–18

JESUS WARNED HIS DISCIPLES to avoid phoniness and hypocrisy.

When I was a child in the 1940s, I spent my summers with my grandparents in San Saba, Texas. After going to the Saturday afternoon movie, I would go to the hardware store where Granddaddy and other ranchers gathered to share stories and talk about cattle and cattle prices. Each summer when the rodeo came to town, if one of the townspeople came in the store wearing a purchased cowboy outfit, the conversation would go something like this:

"I bet he doesn't even know how to hold a rope, much less use one."

"Yeah. But don't he look purrrr-tee."

The ranchers would grin, maybe one or two would chuckle softly; then, they would go back to arguing about the merits of Hereford versus Angus cattle or telling tales about what happened when one of them tangled with an angry bull.

They knew the difference between what they called "a real cow-man" and a drug store cowboy. It was the difference between reality and pretense, between what is authentic and what is phony.

The harshest words that Jesus spoke were addressed to people whose religious lives were such a pretense that they even fooled themselves. Their focus was misplaced and their energies were misdirected. They were failing to live as God intends, and, to add to the tragedy, they were teaching others to do the same.

They were like concert pianists who think that success means being praised for how hard they work on their piano exercises. To be sure, concert pianists invest significant time and energy doing piano exercises, but it is for the purpose of preparing for a concert in which they will make music that feeds the hearts and souls of others.

What finger exercises are to the concert pianist, spiritual disciplines such as prayer and fasting are to the daily living of the faithful. The purpose of such disciplines is to improve one's ability to live the life of faithfulness. To make a show of spiritual disciplines is to miss the point. It is like a concert pianist thinking the goal is to be praised for doing finger exercises, when the true vocation is to bless others with the music of great composers.

Jesus did not discount the importance of spiritual disciplines. He regularly participated in worship at the synagogue on the Sabbath. He frequently sought solitude for prayer. He practiced fasting. He taught us to pray. But for Jesus the true test of faithfulness went well beyond praying and fasting. The true test was in the way he dealt with others, the way he served God through his relationship with others. Just as the purpose of the pianist's finger excercises is to improve the performance of music, spiritual disciplines are for the sake of being more faithful in the midst of daily living.

The impact that God wants us to make on others is not that of impressing them with how skilled and devoted we are to doing our religous exercises. Wanting others to notice our effort and expertise in practicing spiritual disciplines is a sure sign of misdirected faith. Those who make a show of being religious get the payoff they are seeking. People cannot help noticing their perfomance of being religious. But as Jesus pointed out, those who substitute religiosity for faithfulness fail to live by the faith they pretend to have.

Jesus was teaching all who would listen that being a religious show-off is not the way to the fulfillment of the purpose God is offering. God wants servants of divine love, persons who live trusting God so completely that they invest themselves in striving to be servants of God's will. Such people have no need for the applause of the world. Because they are free from requiring the world's approval and appreciation to validate their lives, they are able to be faithful in loving God and neighbor in all they say and do.

There is an inevitable conflict between seeking our own glory and trying to serve God. We may fool others—we may even fool ourselves—but we will not fool God.

"Do not make a show of how hard you are trying to do what God wants," Jesus was saying. "Humbly prepare yourself for the challenges of daily living in obedience to God, and God will empower you to live in harmony with God."

"And when you fast, do not look dismal, like the hypocrites, for they disfigure their faces that their fasting may be seen by men [people]. *Truly, I say to you, they have received their reward. But when you fast, anoint your head and wash your face, that your fasting may not be seen by men* [others] *but by your Father who is in secret; and your Father who sees in secret will reward you"* (Matt 6:16–18).

For Meditation and Conversation

1. What are the forms of religious hypocrisy to which you are most vulnerable?

2. What is your opinion about the hypocrisy of pretending to be less religious than one really is for the sake of social acceptance? To what extent is this hypocrisy a temptation for you?

3. Why do you think Jesus was more vocal in condemnation of hypocrites than other types of sinners?

30

The Real Treasure

JESUS WAS AWARE THAT money is important. Our use of money, our relationship to money, and our attitude toward money are frequent topics in Jesus' teaching. Because our economy does not depend on bartering, money may be even more important now than in Jesus' day, and therefore his wisdom about money even more relevant.

Money is important for us because few of us build our own homes, and even fewer of us grow our own food and make our own clothes. We need money for basic necessities—food, shelther, and clothing. We even need money to give full expression to our love of neighbor. For example, if we want to help people who have lost all their possessions in a hurricane, one of the ways we do that is by giving money so that others can help in ways we are unable to. If we want to help find a cure for cancer or some other disease, the way most of us can help is by providing money to pay the salaries and expenses of those doing research. Money allows us to make a trip to the mountains, or go to a movie, a football game, or a ballet. Money is a necessary tool in the world we live in.

Because money is so important, we are easily seduced into giving it more importance than is appropriate. For some, possessing things and engaging in activities that cost money is what makes life worth living. This is a major factor in the huge amount of personal debt in our society. Many of us want "it" now; we want to enjoy "it" now; we want to do "it" now. So, we put "it" on the credit card and worry about paying for "it" later. Many of us would rather deal with the aggravation of being hounded by bill collectors than not go to an event with friends. Besides, we believe it would be humiliating to let our friends think we could not afford to do what they can.

It is not just our wanting to possess and enjoy some gadget, trip, or activity that lures many of us deeper into debt. We can so enjoy the feeling we experience when we buy something for ourselves or to give a special present to someone we want to impress (spouse, child, friend, or associate) that we spend more than we can afford. Some of us purchase more expensive vehicles than we can afford because we want a car, SUV, or pickup that will fulfill our fantasies, improve our self-images, and/or impress those around us. This type of lifestyle stretches our budget to the breaking point.

It is in this situation that we are most likely to find ourselves feeling resentment when someone asks us to make more than a token gift to support the work of some charity. Rather than examine our values and behavior, we complain that they are always asking for money and find some fault to justify not giving. Meanwhile, our spending and excessive debt continue to cause us stress. Our marriages suffer. Our relationships with our children, with our friends, and with God suffer. We focus on our need to make more money rather than seeing ourselves as having a spiritual problem that has significant ethical implications.

Others of us have a different way of being in bondage to money and possessions. We tenaciously hang on to what we have while working hard to obtain more. We see the debt-driven stress that is distorting the lives of other people, and with pride we say, "Thank God I am not in debt the way they are." Our money is so vital to making us feel secure and comfortable that we are not only unwilling to do anything that might put our financial security at risk, we are also unwilling to share what we have. While we may not be spendthrifts, we are certainly not generous, either.

We who place inordinate importance on our money and possessions tend to be among those made uncomfortable by stories such as the one about the religious young man who asked Jesus, "What good deed must I do to experience the eternal in life?" Jesus told him to keep the commandments. The young man asked, "Which ones?" Jesus said, "Do not kill, do not commit adultery, do not bear false witness, honor [respect and take care of] your parents, and love your neighbor as yourself." The young man's response was, "I've been doing all this. What do I lack?" Jesus then told him to let go of his possessions. "Give all you have to the poor." In other words, invest all you have in serving others. Set yourself free from being in bondage to the things you have and the things you want. The young man was very wealthy, and letting go of his wealth was more than he could bring himself to do. So, as Matthew tells the story, he went away in sadness (Matt 19:16–22).

Money and the use we make of it was important to Jesus. I cannot remember who figured out that if Jesus were a preacher today and spoke of money as often as he did in the four Gospels, one-third of what he had to say (seventeen sermons a year) would focus on our attitude and use of possessions and/or money.

Jesus was aware of how easily money and possessions move from their appropriate place as tools or resources to the place of prominence we reserve for that which shapes our values and behavior. The problem is not that money is evil. Money is merely a resource to be used in living. It allows the carpenter to purchase bread from the baker so that the baker is able to buy shoes for his children.

Jesus was aware that we tend to elevate the importance of money and the things money can buy so that they become the organizing principal in our living. Rather than our lives being shaped by our striving to live as God intends, we drift into attempting to justify our existence by the acquisition of wealth and the things money can buy. Although we deny it with words, Jesus was aware that our behavior often reveals that we confuse the worth of our lives with how much money we make and the monetary value of our various investments.

Even when we have more than enough, we tend to want even more. Public storage is a multibillion-dollar industry in the United States, and it is growing. How many of us are unable to put our car in our garage because it is full of stuff? I am confident that Jesus would interpret such facts as clear evidence of our being a people who are possessed by their possessions. I am convinced that he would see our addiction to wanting more, and our stingily hanging on to all we call "mine," as evidence that we worship the false god of materialism.

Most of us have more than we need, yet most of us give only one or two percent of our income to help those in need. It is clear that all too often our love of our possessions is greater than our love of neighbor; and whenever our love of neighbor is called into question, so is our love of God.

It is not unusual for us to drift into loving our money and possessions more than we love God and neighbor without being aware of making that choice. We did not set out to become greedy and materialistic; we merely want to feel important and enjoy financial security. But one day we wake up believing that we will be happy, successful, and in charge of our lives when we have more money and things. We wear ourselves out trying to obtain more, or find ourselves made angry by requests to share what we have with those in need. Because of our extravgance or our stinginess (or both), our marriages suffer. Our relationships with our children suffer. Our friendships suffer. Sometimes even our health suffers. Most of all, our relationship with God suffers.

We struggle to make money. We lose sleep thinking about how to keep it. We worry about those who may try to take it from us by force or by deception. Some of us are satisfied with the wealth we have obtained, but all too many of us merely run out of time running after more.

If we should happen to look back with perceptive insight, we are likely to see the wreckage of abandoned ideals and the abortion of the good that might have been. We try not to look back (except to see our carefully edited versions of the past). To look back on the way it really was is often too painful—so painful that our subconscious blocks our ability to see the damage that our pursuit of more things has inflicted on others and the possibilities for good that we missed while hanging on to all we call "mine."

Jesus saw the danger. In Matt 6:19–21, he tried to warn anyone who would listen. He told them to be careful in the commitments they make with their resources of time, energy, and money. "Where your treasure is, there will your heart be also." He was saying that where we invest what we have reveals what we truly value in life.

He urged all who would listen not to waste their lives chasing after what does not last. He said, "Do not lay up for yourselves treasures on earth, where moth and rust consume and where thieves break in and steal." He saw the danger and tried to warn them—and us.

More than that, he pointed toward profound meaning, joy, and peace that tragedy and death cannot destroy. "Lay up for yourselves treasures in heaven," he said. He was urging his disciples to focus on living in harmony with God, investing themselves daily in love of God and neighbor.

Jesus' teachings make it clear that we are not going to find the answer to our deepest longings by believing the advertising that is trying to sell us what we do not really need. We must recognize seductive illusions for what they really are—and for what they are not. The way, the truth, and the life that matter are found in following the One who has prepared a place for us in heaven (John 14:1–6).

And where is heaven? It is where God reigns. Heaven is not merely a destination after death; God can reign in the lives of people here and now. "Let the children come to me, and do not hinder them; for to such belongs the kingdom of heaven," Jesus said (Matt 19:14). The kingdom of heaven is where people trust God with the kind of faith with which a little child trusts a loving parent. It is where people embrace the concerns of God—especially the concern for those the world shoves aside. In the kingdom of heaven, faith, hope, and love replace old resentments and fear. The kingdom of heaven is wherever God's forgiveness empowers people to forgive. It is found where those in need are being served (Matt 25:31–36). To be in the kingdom of heaven is to be wherever God reigns and God's will is done—in this life or in the life to come.

The challenge Jesus gave his disciples and anyone who would listen was to examine what they were doing with their time and their money. Such an examination will reveal what they really value and what they really worship.

"Do not lay up for yourselves treasures on earth, where moth and rust consume and where thieves break in and steal, but lay up for yourselves treasures in heaven, where neither moth nor rust consumes and where thieves do not break in and steal. For where your treasure is, there will your heart be also" (Matt 6:19–21).

For Meditation and Conversation

1. What are symptoms of laying up treasures on earth rather than treasures in heaven?

2. What are symptoms of laying up treasures in heaven?

3. What are symptoms of appropriate concern for money?

4. What are symptoms of inappropriate concern for money?

5. What percentage of your income do you use in ways that (you imagine) cause God to smile?

31

The Worst Kind of Blindness

MATTHEW 6:22–23

"WATCH WHERE YOU'RE GOING!" I heard my Grandaddy's words about the same time that I heard and felt the thud of the right front fender of his pickup against a gatepost. He was trying to teach me to drive. As long as he kept that truck, the dent in its right front fender was an embarrassing reminder. I wish I could say that my failure to navigate Grandaddy's pickup through that gate was the only time I failed to watch where I was going.

"Watch where you're going" was one of the lessons that Jesus tried to teach his disciples. Keep your eyes open, he was saying. If you don't keep your eyes open, you will just stumble through life in the dark.

Throughout his ministry, in various ways, Jesus told his disciples to keep the focus of their living on him. "Follow me," he said time after time. If their focus was elsewhere, they would be unable to follow, and the result would be their living in the dark.

The darkness Jesus was talking about is not merely the absence of sunlight, which keeps people from seeing trees and flowers. It is the darkness of soul and heart that falls when we are unable to view life through the eyes of faith. It is the blindness of those whose vision is limited only to what can be measured in a laboratory or calculated by a computer or evaluated by its financial worth.

Just as the darkness of which he spoke was something other than the absence of sunlight, the light of which Jesus spoke was something more.

The first chapter of the Gospel of John declares that this light is at the heart of life. It is the light of God, the light that came among us, as one of us, in Jesus (John 1:1–13).

Speaking the poetry of a profound prophet, Jesus was saying that when we are blind to this light, we live in a darkness greater than any experience of darkness caused by the loss of eyesight. It is a great and terrible darkness because we are not only in the dark, but we are also unaware of being in the dark; and this lack of being aware of our situation is the greatest darkness of all.

Jesus was teaching any who would listen that when we are blind to the light of God, we stumble through life, chasing all sorts of illusions—such as the illusion that laying up more treasures for ourselves will make us persons of worth. When our souls are in the dark, we continue to pursue what we have been chasing, believing that our personal worth is somehow determined by the worth of our assets.

This blind pursuit of what the world around us declares to be the way, the truth, and the life is the kind of living that Jesus said is the result of trying to make it through life with an unsound eye. It is a most tragic kind of blindness, because it is being lost in the darkness and not even knowing that we are in the dark, much less lost.

It was because of this kind of blindness that the religious leaders in Jerusalem failed to see what Jesus was offering, and so they protected what they had by getting rid of him. When we cannot see who Jesus is and what he is offering, we too choose to chase illusions and defensively protect what in ignorance we call "mine" rather than embrace the life he offers. When we consciously or unconsciously reject the life he offers, Christ probably weeps over us, just as he wept over Jerusalem (Luke 19:41).

"The eye is the lamp of the body. So, if your eye is sound, your whole body will be full of light; but if your eye is not sound, your whole body will be full of darkness. If then the light in you is darkness, how great is the darkness!" (Matt 6:22–23)

For Meditation and Conversation

1. What meaning do Jesus' words have for you and your situation?

2. What are symptoms of the darkness Jesus talks about in these verses?

3. What are symptoms of the light Jesus is talking about being in someone?

32

Dealing with Anxiety

MATTHEW 6:24-34

I WONDER HOW MUCH sleep I have lost wrestling with what I call "the midnight crazies"—the various anxieties and worries I can do nothing about at 2 a.m. and, more often than not, little if anything about in the light of day. How many times have I failed to experience the joy of today because I was focused on all that might go wrong tomorrow? How much of my life have I lived like a golfer who plays poorly on this hole because he is worried about the water hazard on the next hole?

Jesus taught all who would listen not to be anxious about tomorrow but to live one day at a time. Yesterday, with its victories and defeats, is gone; tomorrow has not yet arrived. The only life we have is in the present; however, the pain and joy in our past and our fears and hopes about the future make it difficult to stay focused on the present. Wanting to hang on to past happiness, and wanting to avoid heartache and grief, we look for ways to be in control. All around us we see people trying to make life be the way they want by a commitment to the acquisition of wealth, power, or popularity; some of them appear to have achieved their goal, and we are tempted to follow their example.

When we give in to that temptation, we dismiss as nonsense what Jesus taught the disciples about God taking care of us in the way that God takes care of the birds of the air and the lilies of the field. Sweet nonsense, we may say, but nonsense nonetheless. After all, we have seen the TV pictures of children starving and of entire communites that merely happen to be in the wrong place at the wrong time being victimized by terrorism and war. We have seen what happened to friends who did not make adequate financial preparation for their retirement. Because of what we have seen, we tend to ignore what Jesus said about God taking care of the birds of the air and the lilies of the field.

We are realists who have no difficulty understanding the reality of Good Friday. It is Easter that we have trouble believing, and we grow impatient with the promises of the Gospel. In this age of fast foods, we want instant gratification of our desires and quick solutions to our problems. Because the great human problems of war, injustice, cruelty, and hunger continue to rage, we are tempted to view God's promises as a delightful fairy tale that ends, "They lived happily ever after." Wearily we reply, "If only it were true."

We want to believe, yet we live focused on our agenda, confident it is all up to us while at the same time declaring we have faith—just in case. We are semi-secular and semi-believing in our outlook.

"You cannot serve two masters," Jesus told those who would listen. Yet that is what many of us try to do. We want to live as though we are the ones in charge while telling ourselves we have faith in God. But what we frequently mean by "having faith in God" is holding on to the wish-filled dream that God will give us what we want, the way we want it. When life does not fall into place in the way we want it to, we doubt God and God's promises.

Doubting the promises of God, we become more enslaved to our fears and desires. Our worries about what might go wrong tomorrow add to the burdens of today. Focused on what we want to receive tomorrow, we are insensitive to the grace of God at work in our midst today.

Jesus taught the disciples that the way to hope and peace is to strive to do God's will. "Seek first God's kingdom and God's righteousness and all these things shall be yours as well," he said. "Seek first to live under God's reign and in a right relationship with God, then all else will take care of itself" (my paraphrase of Matt 6:33).

But to live this way requires faith in God—trusting God so completely that we strive to sing the song of our life in harmony with God rather than trying to get God to harmonize life to fit the song we want to sing. We are to live trusting the One who is revealed most clearly in the New Testament through Easter.

To have such faith, to live profoundly trusting God in this world where various kinds of crucifixions really do happen, requires a post-Easter vision of God. Whatever else Easter proclaims, it declares to the world that God is not defeated by the worst humans can do. Sin, death, and evil do not have the last word. God does. It was because of their post-Easter understanding of God that the disciples began to grasp what Jesus had been talking about. It is this faith that empowers commitment.

"Seek first the kingdom of God and his righteousness," Jesus said. The kingdom of God is wherever God reigns—be it in this life or in what is beyond death. When Jesus told the disciples to "seek God's kingdom," he was talking about a whole lot more than striving to earn soul-insurance so that when they died they would have earned a reward. He was also talking about their living here and now under God's reign.

To seek "God's righteousness" has to do with striving to live in right relationship with God. "Thou art the potter, I am the clay," Christians have sung.[1] It is the relationship of a trusting child to the ideal, loving Parent (Matt 18:1–4). This is the vision of God that enabled Jesus to pray on the night before the crucifixion, "Father, let this cup pass from me; nevertheless, not my will but yours be done" (Matt 26:39).

Jesus knew the temptation to try to have it both ways. Undoubtedly, he saw then what can be seen today—people focusing primarily on the pursuit of wealth, power, and/or popularity while at the same time wanting a meaningful relationship with God. Of course, when this is the way we live, God is reduced to a supporting role. Then, our relationship with God is primarily one in which we look to God as a resource to help us obtain whatever what *we* want. Rather than striving to discern and do God's will, we try to have a relationship in which God helps us get what we want. In this kind of relationship with God, we are not invested in worshipping God as much as in attempting to manipulate God.

Nowhere in the Bible is wealth in and of itself declared to be evil; the same is true of power and popularity. After all, Solomon was wealthy (1 Kgs 10:14–23), Joseph was powerful (Gen 41:27–45), and David was popular (1 Sam 18:6–9). It's okay, we tell ourselves, to be wealthy, powerful, and popular, and such a statement is true up to a point. But it is one thing to be wealthy; it is another to believe that wealth can make us happy. It is one thing to have power; it is another to believe that power can

---

1. "Have Thine Own Way, Lord"; lyrics by Adelaide A. Pollard.

give us security. It is one thing to be popular; it is another to believe that popularity makes our lives meaningful.

When we begin to live as if wealth, power, and popularity can give us happiness, security, and meaning, we are engaged in what Jesus called "serving mammon." "You cannot serve God and mammon," Jesus was saying to all who would listen (Matt 6:24). As much as we would like it to be otherwise, the truth is that there is no middle ground. We have just so much time and energy, and the way we choose to use our limited time and energy reveals our choice.

The key to profound peace, even in times of conflict and turmoil, is trusting God and God's grace so much that our primary commitment is striving to discern and do God's will. Jesus was teaching the disciples to put first things first. Wealth may or may not come our way. We may or may not have much power (as the world understands power). We may or may not be very popular. According to Jesus, such things are secondary. What truly matters is to seek first to live as God intends. Then, Jesus said, the rest of life will take care of itself.

By the way, it is wise to notice that Jesus was not claiming that his way frees us from all problems. Rather his way is the way we can best deal with our problems—by faith, one day at a time.

"No one can serve two masters; for either he will hate the one and love the other, or he will be devoted to the one and despise the other. You cannot serve God and mammon. Therefore I tell you, do not be anxious about your life, what you shall eat or what you shall drink, nor about your body, what you shall put on. Is not your life more than food, and the body more than clothing? Look at the birds of the air: they neither sow nor reap nor gather into barns, and yet your heavenly Father feeds them. Are you not of more value than they? And which of you by being anxious can add one cubit to his span of life [or stature]? And why are you anxious about clothing? Consider the lilies of the field, how they grow; they neither toil nor spin; yet I tell you, even Solomon in all his glory was not arrayed like one of these. But if God so clothes the grass of the field, which today is alive and tomorrow is thrown into the oven, will he not much more clothe you, O men [people] of little faith? Therefore do not be anxious, saying, 'What shall we eat?' or 'What shall we drink?' or 'What shall we wear?' For the Gentiles seek all these things; and your heavenly Father knows that you need them all. But seek first his kingdom and his righteousness, and all these things shall be yours as well. Therefore do not be anxious about tomorrow, for tomorrow

will be anxious for itself. Let the day's own trouble be sufficient for the day" (Matt 6:24–34).

For Meditation and Conversation

1. What meaning and implications do you discern in Jesus' statement, "You cannot serve God and mammon"?

2. In what ways are you tempted to serve more than one master?

3. From what Jesus said about our not being anxious, what did you learn about how to live without anxiety?

33

On Being Judgmental

MATTHEW 7:1-5

THE MAN'S DISGUST WAS flavored with anger as he talked about the way that some of the people with whom he worked were two-faced and how they failed in their responsibilities. What I learned sometime later was that at the time that he was displaying his angry disgust regarding the behavior of some of his colleagues, he was being unfaithful to his wife and children in an ongoing affair with another woman.

"Why do you see the speck that is in your neighbor's eye, but do not notice the log that is in your own?" Jesus asked.

Jesus was aware that we humans can be so focused on the sin of others that we become insensitive to our own sin, which makes it easy for our sinfulness to expand. The history of human conflict has many examples of individuals, groups, and nations who have been so caught up in their passionate fight against some form of evil or injustice that their zeal led them into behavior similar to the evil they were fighting. At the beginning of World War II, the people of Great Britain and the United States were filled with moral outrage by the Nazis bombing of civilian populations. By the end of that war, the majority of the people in both nations supported bombings that started firestorms that caused the death of thousands of German and Japanese civilians.

"Why do you see the speck that is in your neighbor's eye, but do not notice the log that is in your own?" Jesus asked. It is easy for me to condemn someone who pretends to be more religious than he or she really is. Religious hypocrisy not only offends me, it makes me angry. And yet, as I mentioned earlier, all too often I engage in another form hypocrisy— secular hypocrisy. Secular hypocrisy is most tempting when I am in social or civic settings outside the church community. I can be so afraid that someone will write me off because I am religious that I pretend to be less religious than I really am. I do not believe I am alone. To be sure, secular hypocrisy is more acceptable in our society than religious hypocrisy, but phoniness is phoniness, hypocrisy is hypocrisy, regardless of whether its nature is religious or secular.

"Why do you see the speck that is in your neighbor's eye, but do not notice the log that is in your own?" Jesus asked. "First take the log out of your own eye, and then you will see clearly to take the speck out of your neighbor's eye" (Matt 7:1–5).

Jesus was teaching his disciples while others listened that "until you are aware of your own need for God's grace, you will be less than effective as an instrument of God's life-transforming grace in the lives of others." As long as we are in denial of our own sin, our efforts to deal with the sin of others will be less than redemptive.

"Hate the sin, but love the sinner," is an often repeated admonition. But as another familiar phrase puts it, "Easier said than done." The more we take pride in our virtue, the more difficult it is to love the sinner. Our arrogant denial of our own need for mercy adds fuel to the fire of our being judgmental of others.

It is humble recognition of our own sin and our own need for redeeming grace that helps keep us from making self-righteous judgments about other people. When we know our need for merciful grace, we tend to be sensitive to that need in others.

When we are aware of our need for forgiveness, we are open to receive it. Then, as we receive God's grace, grace shapes the way we deal with our neighbor. We are able to see not only the wrong the neighbor has done but also to see, or at least trust, that there is potential for good in the neighbor. This insight makes it possible for us to be merciful.

One of the well-known stories about Jesus is the one in which some religious leaders try to trap him by bringing him a woman who had been caught committing adultery (John 8:3–10). The law was clear; she was to be put to death (Lev 20:10 and Deut 22:22). By the way, that law also condemned the man, but he obviously was not brought before Jesus. The religious leaders asked Jesus what he had to say about this woman. His response was, "Let him who is without sin among you cast the first stone." The passage in John states that all her accusers left one by one, "beginning with the oldest." This comment reflects a keen insight about life, because the longer we live (if we have any insight and honesty at all) the more we are aware of our own lack of perfection and our need for forgiveness. When Jesus was the only one left who could accuse her, he said to the woman, "Neither do I condemn you; go, and do not sin again."

Jesus did not condone or ignore the woman's sin. But his focus was on redemption, not revenge. His understanding of justice focused on the way life is intended to be rather than on carrying out legalized punishment for past failures.

Jesus knew that when our hearts have not been transformed by God's love, we tend to take excessive pride in being right and doing good, and we tend to be harsh in our judgment of others. We will even try to justify our harshness by telling ourselves that we are just doing it for their own good. Sometimes we will even dare to say that we are doing it in the name of God.

When, in our self-righteous pride, we are made aware of our faults and failures, we tend to look for someone to blame. Pridefully avoiding responsibility for our failure, we find it easy to almost take pleasure in the faults and failures of others. Perhaps our indulgence in standing in judgment of others is a way of feeling superior. To protect our distorted self-image, we indulge in a variety of excuses for ourselves and avoiding responsibility for our sin and shortcomings: "It is because of my bad experiences in childhood." "It is because what he did was so hurtful that I had to respond the way I did." "If she had just done X, I would never have done Y."

The divine love we see in Jesus stands in sharp contrast to behavior that is judgmental, self-righteous, and loveless. In the floodlight of Christ's love, the truth about ourselves that we have tried to hide from God, from others, and most of all from ourselves, stands nakedly revealed. "Judge not, that you be not judged," Jesus said to his disciples.

It is in losing ourselves in the love of God and neighbor that we discover who we really are and who we are meant to be. To live such a life is not to stand in a position of superiority, looking down and being judgmental, but rather to approach each neighbor as Jesus approached each person.

This certainly does not mean that we remain silent in the face of evil or sit passively idle in the face of injustice. Love speaks the tough words of truth. But our words and deeds of tough love are not those of the self-righteous judge passing sentence. Our words and deeds are those of sinners who know they continually live their lives needing the undeserved gift of forgiveness; yet because of the claims of grace on their lives, their commitment to justice and mercy will not allow them to remain silent and do nothing. When words and deeds are appropriate expressions of tough love that hold others accountable for the wrong that has been done, the words and deeds are expressions of concern and compassion rather than reflections of pride or arrogance. The goal of tough love is transformation rather than revenge. (See comments regarding forgiveness in chapter 25, which treats Matt 6:12, and chapter 28, which treats Matt 6:14–15.)

Jesus was teaching all who would listen that it is God's grace flowing through us that enables us to be instruments of God's love, making the world whole. To be less and to do less is to become tools of the devil.

"Judge not, that you be not judged. For with the judgment you pronounce you will be judged, and the measure you give will be the measure you get. Why do you see the speck that is in your brother's eye, but do not notice the log that is in your own eye? Or how can you say to your brother, 'Let me take the speck out of your eye,' when there is the log in your own eye? You hypocrite, first take the log out of your own eye, and then you will see clearly to take the speck out of your brother's [neighbor's] *eye"* (Matt 7:1–5).

For Meditation and Conversation

1. What implications for yourself do you discern in Jesus saying, "with the judgment you pronounce you will be judged, and the measure you give will be the measure you get"?

2. What meaning have you found in Jesus' comments about the speck and the log?

3. As we wrestle with the temptation to be judgmental, what is our hope?

34

Don't Be Naive

MATTHEW 7:6

WHEN JESUS TAUGHT, HE was not merely focused on what he wanted to say but also on the people to whom he was speaking. I am convinced that this focus on people is why he warned his disicples not to give dogs what is holy and not to throw pearls to pigs. He was urging them not to waste their opportunities to share the Gospel. They should know and care about the people to whom they are talking so that when they share the Gospel with them, they do so in ways that are most likely to allow the Gospel to make it into the hearts and minds of those to whom they are speaking.

In the Sermon on the Mount, it is evident that Jesus loved the people so much that his teaching or preaching technique was chosen with the goal of the message being heard. Jesus was not merely focused on what he was saying but also on how to say it. As the first verses of Matt 5 make clear, when he saw the multitude coming, he chose not to address the crowd directly. Instead he taught his disciples in such a way that the multitude could overhear what he was teaching. It seems that he chose to use indirect communication as a strategy for getting past the defensiveness of the listeners and into their hearts and minds (see chapter 2). Sometimes we are so focused on expressing our message in some ideal way that we ignore the question of what is the most effective way to communicate the meaning of what we are saying.

I remember my response to an insensitive, evangelistic Christian who confronted me when I was a sophomore in college. We had just been introduced when he glared into my eyes and, with great intensity and no trace of compassion, asked, "Are you saved?" He probably thought he was being forceful for the sake of the Gospel. But to me he seemed self-righteously judgmental and playing to the audience of other church members nearby. I remember thinking at the time, "You don't care beans about me; you just want bragging rights for saving another soul." I imagined his Bible cover being like the fuselage of a World War II fighter, but instead of painting a little flag for each enemy plane shot down, he pasted the decal of a human figure to keep track of the number of souls he had "saved."

Looking back, I know the question he asked me was one I needed to wrestle with at that point in my life. But I responded negatively to what seemed to be an arrogant, self-righteous, and condescending hard-sell approach. Today, I would like to believe his intention was to share in a forceful way what had been been intensely meaningful and influential in his own life. However, he was so focused on and committed to his way of thinking and talking about the Gospel that he took no time to get to know who I was, much less care about my concerns, questions, and needs. He was so in love with his mission to save souls, and perhaps so naive as to think that his way of sharing the Gospel was the only way, that he failed to express the least amount of genuine concern for me as a person. I would like to believe that his intention was to express his love for God; however, in his actions and words, he totally failed to communicate any concern for this neighbor.

Rather than help me experience grace and grow in grace, he merely confirmed what was, at that point in my life, a growing cynicism about church people. Back then I would have said, "Church folks may talk about love of God and neighbor, but they do not care about persons. What they are really interested in is being praised for success in pressuring others to recite specified religious phrases and join their religious club."

He reinforced my cynical view rather than influencing me toward a more positive view. In that man's misguided zeal, he had thrown pearls into the mud of my pig pen and wasted his opportunity to be a positive influence in leading me to grow in grace and mature in faith.

"Don't be naive," Jesus was saying to his disciples. To share the Gospel takes more than words passionately spoken. The Gospel message is too precious to be handled carelessly. Do not throw it out like scraps thrown to the dogs; do not take this precious pearl and throw it into a pig pen to be trampled into the mud. Jesus was not trying to halt or limit his disciples in sharing the Gospel. Remember what Jesus said at the end of the book of Matthew about sharing the gospel with all the world? Jesus wanted his disciples to share boldly but not naively. He did not want them to waste their opportunies to make a difference in the lives of others.

Earlier Jesus had told the disciples that in dealing with people, they were to avoid hypocrisy. Now he was urging them to be careful with their sincerity in sharing the good news of God's grace with others. This being careful is not the carefulness of being overly cautious but rather the care-full-ness of striving to express the gospel in such way that their words and deeds did not get in the way of God's grace. They were to take care, lest their attempts to share the Gospel were as counterproductive as the efforts of the evangelistic Christian who gave me the insensitive hard sell.

There are few things in life more intoxicating than the excitement of having a positive, life-shaping experience—the excitement of discovering truth that ignites within us hope and joy while giving us a sense of purpose and meaning. There are few urges stronger than the urge to share such a wonderful experience with someone else. Jesus was aware of this urge to share, and he was teaching his disciples to be careful in their sharing.

He knew that when novices with more enthusiasm than wisdom try to share with others what they have discovered, the result can be worse than merely disappointing. When they find themselves and their message angrily rejected, some rookie disciples withdraw from sharing what they long to share. Fear of being made fun of has silenced all too many followers of Jesus and lured them into the hypocrisy of pretending to be less faithful than they really are.

The response of other rookie disciples is not fearful withdrawal but anger and a strong desire to bring shame or pain to those who rejected them and what they offered: "How dare you laugh! How dare you reject the Truth!" Because they are hurt, they slip from the righteousness that is being in a right relationship with God into a self-righteousness in which they are less concerned about being faithful to God than they are with defending what they said and did, and attacking those who rejected their effort.

There is yet another reason to be careful in sharing the gospel. There are those who, in ignorance or self-centeredness, will grab hold of all that is sacred and twist it into some sort of pretend magic that serves their selfishness. Then, in the name of the gospel, they go about distorting the gospel. They will take the gosple and gut it, throwing away the parts that bother them and magnifying out of proportion those parts that seem to serve their narrow self-interest. They will trample into the mud the pearls of the gospel in their attempt to have it be what they want it to be. They will embrace God's grace—but only as another resource for making life be what they want life to be. They will twist and distort all that is holy for the sake of having their modified "gospel" get them what they want, bless their special group's goals or their nation's policies. In this, they desecrate what is holy and trample the pearls of the gospel.

More than once in the history of Christianity, the longing of religious people to see their nation as a Christian nation has seduced them into condoning distortions of the gospel for the sake of nationalistic expediency and power. Or, longing to believe their business reflects the values of Christ, they try to turn Jesus into their business partner who will help them obtain the kind of success that they want and that the world rewards. But, of course, Jesus did not come to be our partners in helping us get what we want, but rather he came to transform us so that we are his partners in doing what God wants.

Our desire to have everyone embrace the gospel can seduce us into another way of treating the gospel like a pearl thrown into a pig pen to be trampled into the mud until it disappears from view. In our desire to have everyone embrace the gospel, we are tempted to water down what is holy. Longing for everyone to agree, we can drift toward tolerating distortions of truth and destructive living. Meanwhile, those whom we have tried to embrace with a tolerance that has no boundary lines, continue to have no more regard for God's grace and God's will revealed in Jesus Christ than swine have for pearls trampled in the mud.

Earlier in Matthew, Jesus warned the disciples against being judgmental, but here he warns them about being naive in sharing the good news about God's love and the implications of this gospel.

"Do not give dogs what is holy; and do not throw your pearls before swine, lest they trample them underfoot and turn to attack you" (Matt 7:6).

For Meditation and Conversation

1. What are some ways that you have observed followers of Jesus

"giving dogs what is holy" and "throwing pearls to the pigs," and what was your reaction?

2. Of the various ways to be naive and wasteful in striving to share the gospel, which are the ones you have to be most on guard against?

3. What do you need to do or not do in order to prevent yourself from being naive and wasteful in your witness?

35

You Can Do It

MATTHEW 7:7–14

WHAT JESUS WAS TEACHING his disciples was and is a tall order. Earnestly seek God and strive to do God's will. Love your neighbor, including your enemies. Don't be a religious show-off when you do good deeds or when you pray. Don't be a hypocrite, and do not be naive in sharing your faith.

An understandable question would have been: Who can live such a life? Jesus, therefore, went on to tell them that they *could* do it. To be able to live each day as God intends, all they had to do was to ask and it would be given, to seek and they would find, to knock and the door would be opened to them.

Obviously, the kind of asking, seeking, and knocking Jesus was talking about is the kind of asking, seeking, and knocking that is consistent with all that he had said up to that point. He was not urging them to behave like pampered children in a toy store: begging, demanding, and expecting their mother to give them whatever they wanted. He was speaking to those whose goal was to live the kind of blessed life Jesus had been talking about since the beginning of the Sermon on the Mount.

"You can do it," is what he was saying. "God will help you."

Nothing undercuts the life of faith more than the loss of hope, the feeling that the ideal is so ideal that there is no hope of our attaining it. Nothing undercuts commitment more than the perception that our efforts are doomed always to be something between inadequate and fail-ing. Faithfulness becomes anemic in the absence of hope.

"There *is* hope," Jesus was saying to any who would listen. In effect, he was telling them: You can be the persons God intends you to be. In your daily living, you can achieve the proper balance between letting your light shine before others and not throwing pearls into the mud of a pig pen. God will enable you to say what needs saying and to do what needs doing. You can live lives of compassion in the midst of those who do not care and among those whose selfishness leads them to take advantage of your compassion.

The key is in asking, seeking, and knocking. These are the keys to both faith and hope; therefore they are essential to living lives shaped by God's grace. You have to want it, Jesus was saying, really want it. We are to ask. We are to pray for ourselves and for others.

We are to seek. We are to do more than passively beg. We are to search for the answers to our deeper questions. We have been given tools for seeking: the community of faith, the heritage of Christian wisdom, the Scriptures, services of worship, the Lord's Supper, examples of true faith-fulness, the gift of prayer, and the ability to meditate on the Word. But, of course, tools are only tools. Hammers and saws do not build houses—car-penters do. There are resources to aid us in seeking, but we are the ones who must do the seeking.

We are to knock. Persistence and perseverance are essential, espe-cially in hard times, when life is like crucifixion. In such a time, even Jesus felt God-forsaken (Mark 15:34). But we are to persist, like the widow who would not let the judge rest until justice was done (Luke 18:1–8). Only God knows why sometimes it takes such a long time for the will of God to be done. We are to stand at the door and knock. We dare not walk away too soon, declaring that no one is home. We are to be persistent. We are to knock until the door is opened, until we too are welcomed into the Father's house. With the persistence of Jacob, who refused to let go of the special agent of God with whom he wrestled in the darkness until he had been blessed by the ordeal, so we also are to hang on for the blessing that is promised (Gen 32:22–32).

Jesus was speaking to the disciples—to those who were committed to following him, and to anyone else who would listen. The kind of life he was talking about is not easy, but he assured them that God will provide what is needed to live such a life. All they (or we) have to do is ask, seek, and knock—that is, *really want* that kind of life and actively implore God to help.

Jesus promised that God will not turn his back. Jesus reminded the disciples that if imperfect, sinful parents, who do harm as the result of their ignorance and sin, are able to do good for their children, then God, who is the ideal Parent, will certainly provide what is needed.

Jesus assured his listeners that there is hope. It is possible to live our daily lives loving God with all that we are and our neighbors as ourselves. All we must do is really want such a life—want it so much that we ask, seek and knock.

And in the process of being able to live as God intends, we will also receive the bonus of what Paul called the fruit of the Spirit (gifts of God): love, joy, peace, patience, kindness, goodness, faithfulness, gentleness, self-control (Gal 5:22–23).

"Ask, and it will be given you; seek, and you will find; knock, and it will be opened to you. For every one who asks receives, and he who seeks finds, and to him who knocks it will be opened. Or what man of you, if his son asks him for bread, will give him a stone? Or if he asks for a fish, will give him a serpent? If you then, who are evil, know how to give good gifts to your children, how much more will your Father who is in heaven give good things to those who ask him!" (Matt 7:7–14)

For Meditation and Conversation

In order to access the grace of God that will empower and enable you to live as God intends you to live:

1. How do you "ask," and what is given you?

2. How do you "seek," and what is it you find?

3. How do you "knock," and what is opened to you?

36

The Golden Rule

MATTHEW 7:12

"Do unto others as you would have them do unto you," Jesus taught his disciples. This golden rule is so obviously true that it is found in almost every culture and religion in one form or another. It is so profound that its implications for ethics have filled libraries. In this statement is the essence of both justice and mercy. Jesus said all that the law and the prophets have to say about our dealing with one another is summed up in this statement. It is the key to ideal relationships.

To treat others when they are right the way that we want to be treated when we are right, and to treat others when they are wrong the way that we want to be treated when we are wrong, sounds simple. One would think it would be the basic rule that shapes the daily living of everyone. But the painful truth reflected in the latest TV news or in our most honest memoirs reveals that we humans all too often ignore or reject the wisdom of this golden rule.

Our motivation to do unto others as we would have them do unto us all too easily evaporates when we are dealing with strangers, foreigners, or rivals. We take refuge in the slogan "Let the buyer beware." After all, we have been taught that the name of the game is winning or making a profit. Having experienced exploitation, we tell ourselves, "We had better do *it* to them before they do *it* to us."

In dealing with those who have hurt us, we are tempted to pervert the wisdom in this command by turning it around to justify our hurting them as they have hurt us. We do unto them as they did to us rather than doing as we would have them do.

Even when we are trying to fulfill this golden rule, and our desire to justify revenge is not present, we humans have a tendency to distort the wisdom in this saying through ignorance and subconscious egotism. It is easy to assume that everyone is just like I am, with my set of fears and hopes, tastes and desires. We humans easily forget that the other person or the other group really is *other*. All too often, without realizing what we have done, we treat the other person as if she or he is an extension or reflection of ourselves. Then, we choose for a birthday present the toy we want to play with, the book we want to read, the music we want to hear. When we are insensitive to the *otherness* of the other and blind to our differences, we distort the deceptively simple wisdom of doing to and for others as we want them to do to and for us.

Why are we humans so often insensitive to the *otherness* of the other person? Why is the obvious wisdom of this golden rule so often distorted? It is so obviously true and profoundly simple; why is it so often ignored or rejected?

The law and the prophets alone could not make genuine compassion for the other person happen. It takes more than eloquent expressions of "you ought to" or "you should" to get us to do what we ought to do and to be who we should be. It takes the power of God.

It is only as God's divine love that was incarnate in Jesus flows into us that it can flow through us. It is in being loved and opening ourselves to God's love that we are enabled to love. When the kind of love we see in Jesus flows through our living, our compassion and our confidence in the grace of God overpowers the fear that tends to drive and distort our living. It is in trusting and embracing the love that has its ultimate source in God that we are set free to live our lives doing works of mercy and justice—that is, we are able to live the life that this simple command calls for.

"So whatever you wish that men [people] *would do to you, do so to them; for this is the law and the prophets"* (Matt 7:12).

For Meditation and Conversation

1. What do you think are the primary reasons that the profound wisdom of this simple statement is frequently ignored?

2. Which of the reasons for ignoring this golden rule are especially tempting to you?

3. What enables or empowers you to have your living shaped by this summary statement of the law and the prophets?

37

The Narrow Gate

MATTHEW 7:13–14

TO EXPERIENCE DAILY LIVING as God intends, Jesus told his disciples, "Enter by the narrow gate." Whatever else he meant, obviously he was not advocating that we do whatever we please or whatever everyone else is doing. One of the most popular illusions regarding the way to happiness is that we will be happy when we can do or have whatever we want, whenever we want, wherever we want. However, Jesus was calling for a specific way of living.

The essence of this way of living was summed up in the two commandments that Jesus and his religious opponents agreed are the most important: to love God with all we are and to love our neighbors as ourselves (Matt 22:34–40; Deut 6:5; Lev 19:18).

We are to center and ground our daily living in the love of God. Rather than using and abusing others, we are to treat them in the way that we want to be treated. Rather than fighting evil with evil (that is, tearing down and tearing apart in an attempt to end tearing down and tearing apart), we are to do the more difficult and costly work of responding to evil with good—that is, being constructive in the midst of destruction (Rom 12:21).

This response is not the popular way. The popular way to respond to being hurt by others is to strike back, inflicting greater pain. The most popular approach to daily living is doing what we want when we want, pursuing what will bring us whatever we want, be it pleasure, status, prestige, popularity, wealth, power, recognition, or some combination of these desires. Those who get in our way are to be craftily manipulated or run over. But this popular way of living leads to injustice, discord, hostility, and revenge begetting revenge—the inevitable by-products of self-centered living. It is not unusual for people who think of themselves as being faithful to embrace this futile and destructive way of living.

When this self-centered way of living is called into question, often the response is one of the following: "If you do not take care of yourself and those you care about, who will?" "Look out for number one." "It is a dog-eat-dog world." "Life is short; get what you can while the getting is good." "If you do not blow your own horn, who will?" "Everybody else is doing it; why not?" "We have grown beyond the primitive notions of heaven and hell. Do what you please." "If God is, and if God really does love me, then God wants me to be happy; and since 'this' is what will make me happy, 'this' must be God's will for me." "After all I have been through, I have the right to do what I am doing." This highway is wide and well traveled; that is why it is so hard to believe that it leads to destruction.

Meanwhile, various forms of subtle and blatant selfishness, fear, and greed cause persons to take advantage of individuals, and groups to dominate other groups, and the planet to be plundered for profit at the expense of future generations. The anxieties of wealthy individuals and nations grow while the anger and frustration of poor individuals and nations increase. In the midst of this complex situation of greed and frustration, there sometimes comes an uneasy silence, in which the poets hear time bombs ticking, and out-of-date, out-of-style prophets warn us of the wrath to come.

Jesus said it is the minority who hear, and even fewer believe. Few travel the road believing that it is blessed to be poor in spirit, to mourn, to be meek, to hunger and thirst for righteousness, to be merciful, to be pure in heart, to be peacemakers, to be persecuted for righteousness' sake. Few people believe that this is the way to heaven, the way to living now and forever in communion with God. Many people are religious, Jesus said, but relatively few are faithful enough to choose this path through the wilderness of life.

From the perspective of those captive to a materialistic society in which self-centeredness is assumed and self-fulfillment viewed as a virtue, the gate to the fulfillment that God intends seems to be unbelievably narrow. It seems to be an impossible way of daily living. Left to ourselves, our weakness and fears will defeat us. Yet if we focus on following Jesus one step at a time, one moment at a time, we can do it.

The question that is most helpful is not whether we will live the rest of our lives in the way that God wants us to live but rather to ask moment by moment whether we will take the next step in this way of daily living.

The gospel, the Good News, is that by God's grace, we can—one step at a time.

"Enter by the narrow gate; for the gate is wide and the way is easy, that leads to destruction, and those who enter by it are many. For the gate is narrow and the way is hard, that leads to life, and those who find it are few" (Matt 7:13–14).

For Meditation and Conversation

1. What do you think is the destruction that comes from choosing what Jesus called the wide gate and the easy way?

2. What do you think Jesus meant when he said, "The gate is narrow and the way is hard, that leads to life, and those who find it are few"?

3. What implications do you see in this passage for your daily living?

38

Beware of Wolves

MATTHEW 7:15-20

"WATCH OUT!" JESUS WARNED the disciples and all who would listen. There are some people who, in the name of God, will invite you on a life journey that moves away from God. Sometimes they are con artists, persons whose conscience is not bothered by taking advantage of the trust you give them. Some of these people seek recognition; others want your money, and still others simply enjoy manipulating people to do their bidding. These are false prophets who know they are false and are not bothered by that knowledge.

Often false prophets are insensitive to the lie they are living and proclaiming. These false prophets are deceived as well as deceiving. They are earnest, devout, and even zealous in their commitment. To those who live passionless lives, the seemingly earnest sincerity of these misled and misleading leaders is winsome. Those who are longing for some sense of purpose and importance are tempted to follow them, seduced by the intensity of their commitment.

Sometimes, in their efforts to proclaim the love of God, what they proclaim is the illusion that there is a surefire way to manipulate God to give us whatever our hearts desire—money for whatever we want, acclaim to overcome our feelings of insecurity, or never being sad or unhappy again. Sometimes what they proclaim taps into feelings of guilt and the often accompanying longing to be holier than others. Sometimes what they preach plays on the fears of the listeners and appeals to their prejudices. John Calvin was right when he wrote that we humans not only have a propensity toward falsehood, we also have a natural desire to be deceived, and are quite ingenious in deceiving ourselves.[1]

When Jesus said, "Beware," it was a warning, like the sign that alerts us that a road may be "slippery when wet." It is not a declaration to make us fearful or anxious, merely appropriately cautious. It is a warning not to be gullible when others seem to be offering us some sort of pot of gold at the end of the rainbow they want us to chase.

"By their fruits you will know them," Jesus said. We are to be at least as careful as when buying a used car. Learn where it has been and what it has been through. Check to see if there is enough power in the engine for the long journey ahead, and whether or not there is rust and rot under the fancy paint job.

If the Bible is quoted, are the verses chosen consistent with the message of the Bible as a whole? Are the selected verses clear and plain in their meaning, and are they consistent with the two laws that Jesus declared are most important (to love God with all we are and our neighbor as ourselves)? Does the kind of living being urged bear the fruit of which Paul wrote: love, joy, patience, kindness, goodness, faithfulness, gentleness, self-control (Gal 5:22–23)? Does their teaching influence persons away from the self-centered love that society proclaims and toward the self-giving love of God and neighbor that Jesus proclaimed? Does what they say and do put into practice what Jesus taught?

If so, what they have to offer is the real thing—the authentic Word, the good news. But if what they preach does not bear the kind of fruit that is consistent with the teachings of Jesus, if what they teach does not bear the fruit of the Spirit that Paul described, it does not pass the test, and then it is merely refuse to be thrown in garbage dump fires.

"Beware of false prophets, who come to you in sheep's clothing but inwardly are ravenous wolves. You will know them by their fruits. Are grapes gathered from thorns, or figs from thistles? So, every sound tree bears good fruit, but the bad tree bears evil fruit. A sound tree cannot bear evil fruit, nor can a bad tree bear good fruit. Every tree that does not bear good fruit is cut down and thrown into the fire. Thus you will know them by their fruits" (Matt 7:15–20).

---

1. Calvin, *A Harmony of the Synoptic Gospels*, 159.

For Meditation and Conversation

1. What do you think are some of the characteristics of false prophets who claim to speak for God in our society?

2. What tempts us to follow false prophets?

3. What tempts us to be false prophets?

4. What are the characteristics of faithful prophets in our time?

5. What encourages and empowers us to be more like them?

39

It Takes More than Merely Being Religious

MATTHEW 7:21–27

FOR OUR LIVING TO be as God intends it to be requires more than at-tending worship, being proud of one's piety and eloquent in public prayer. It takes more than talking church talk. It requires more than do-ing obviously religious deeds. Jesus told all who would listen: "Not every one who says to me, 'Lord, Lord,' shall enter the kingdom of heaven, but he who does the will of my Father who is in heaven. On that day many will say to me, 'Lord, Lord, did we not prophesy in your name, and cast out demons in your name, and do many mighty works in your name?' And then will I declare to them, 'I never knew you; depart from me, you evildoers'" (Matt 7:21–23).

The daily living that Jesus was talking about is not merely saying the right religious words and doing specified holy deeds. He called for liv-ing in a trusting, obedient relationship with God, continually striving to discern God's will and earnestly trying to do it. One who does this in his or her daily living is blessed, Jesus said. (See chapters 3–11 of this book, which treat the beatitudes.)

From what Jesus teaches, it is evident that sincere effort rooted in the pure intention to love God and neighbor is more pleasing to God than outward religious accomplishments done merely out of habit or for recognition. The curve by which God grades baffles the high achievers, who take great pride in their accomplishments. God's honor role is deter-mined not by our saying certain words and doing certain deeds but rather by what we honor, what we value—the intention and purpose that shapes the words and deeds of our daily living.

To the hardheaded pragmatists of the world, it may seem foolish to value intentions over results. It is not that God is unconcerned with results; God cares, but God's concern is not merely with the results of what we say and do, but also (and most especially) with the intention motivating what we say and do, and the values shaping our daily living. God's concern is for us and for who we really are. The Lord sees through our words and deeds to discern what has captured our hearts and what we really worship through our daily living.

When God examines our lives, God is something like a building inspector who knows where to look to determine whether or not the house can endure the storms that attack our souls. God is not fooled by the exterior design, nor by the interior decorating. The Lord has been in the business a long time. He knows all the tricks we humans have used to deceive others and most especially ourselves. "What is it all built upon?" he asks. "Is it built on the high ground, or will it be overwhelmed by the floodwaters of life? Can it endure the hurricane-force winds of tragedy that sooner or later blow through each life?"

There is a wide variety of faulty foundations, inappropriate values, and distorted desires. Some people value recognition and appreciation; they consciously and unconsciously try to use Christ and the gospel to obtain what their hearts desire. Some value power and respect; they consciously and unconsciously try to use Christ and the gospel to obtain what their hearts desire. Some value comfort and security; they consciously and unconsciously try to use Christ and the gospel to obtain what their hearts desire.

When the storms come, our values and desires are tested. The Lord has seen people whose outward lives are like beautiful houses that fall apart in the storms, even though in fair weather they had received recognition and been declared models to copy. They fell apart because they were not built on the solid foundation of faith in and commitment to God and God's grace. Their lives were built on something else, and that something else was like sand when the storms came.

Jesus knew what it takes to endure the storms and crosses of life. It takes more than knowing the right words to recite and doing the proper deeds. It is what the words and deeds are built on that ultimately makes the difference when the storms of life are raging. The words and the deeds of daily livng are to be rooted in and motivated by striving to have one's daily living reflect the compassion, wisdom, and truth that Jesus pointed toward in this his most famous sermon.

"Not every one who says to me, 'Lord, Lord,' shall enter the kingdom of heaven, but he who does the will of my Father who is in heaven. On that day many will say to me, 'Lord, Lord, did we not prophesy in your name, and cast out demons in your name, and do many mighty works in your name?' And then will I declare to them, 'I never knew you; depart from me, you evildoers.' Every one then who hears these words of mine and does them will be like a wise man who built his house upon the rock; and the rain fell, and the floods came, and the winds blew and beat upon that house, but it did not fall, because it had been founded on the rock. And every one who hears these words of mine and does not do them will be like a foolish man who built his house upon the sand; and the rain fell, and the floods came, and the winds blew and beat against that house and it fell; and great was the fall of it" (Matt 7:21–27).

For Meditation and Conversation

1. What do you think is the signifiance of Jesus' warning the disciples that not everyone who says, "Lord, Lord," or speaks in Jesus' name, or does good deeds in Jesus' name will enter the kingdom of heaven, in this life or in the life to come?

2. What are symptoms seen in the daily living of those who have heard and embraced what Jesus was talking about?

3. To what extent do you think your life is like a house built on a rock? What experiences in living make you think so?

40

Response to the Sermon

MATTHEW 7:28–29

WHEN JESUS FINISHED HIS sermon, Matthew tells us that those who had heard what he had said were amazed. Jesus did not sound like other religious leaders of his day. He spoke with an authority unlike the authority of scholars (scribes). His authority was more than knowledge and verbal skills. He spoke wisdom and truth that the people recognized as being rooted in something greater than a high IQ and a formal education.

The authority with which Jesus spoke reflected who he was—the embodiment of God's grace and truth. This authority is that of a true servant of God. It is the authority Jesus described to his disciples when they were vying for positions of importance: "Whoever would be great among you, that person must be your servant; even as the Son of man came not to be served but to serve, and to give his life as a ransom for many" (Matt 20:25–28; Mark 10:42–45; Luke 22:25–27).

His servant-leadership was evident from the beginning of his ministry. In the verses prior to this sermon, Matthew told his readers that Jesus had been teaching in synagogues in Galilee and healing people. Because of his effectiveness, news about Jesus spread throughout the region, and people from beyond Galilee were among those who came to him for help (Matt 4:23–25). The authority Jesus possessed was the authority of a servant—the consummate servant of God. Because Jesus personified this authority in what he taught through word and deed, when the Sermon on the Mount came to an end, the people were amazed. They sensed that he was different from other religious leaders.

As I try to imagine the scene when Jeus stopped speaking, I imagine there being silence. The people were spellbound. They had not merely heard some interesting ideas and helpful suggestions that they could think about, talk about, and debate. They had experienced an encounter with the grace and truth of God, and they had no words for that experience. In time, the faithful would understand that Jesus was the incarnation of God and God's grace. As they began to move from that hillside, I imagine first one and then another saying, "I've never had such an experience! Have you ever heard such a man?"

What comes next to my mind is a question not asked by Matthew. What are the people who had been listening to Jesus going to do in response to his teachings? For us, the more pertinent question is, What are we going to do?

Taking seriously what Jesus said can be intimidating. It can feel so intimidating that some people who think of themselves as being religious will substitute beliefs about Jesus and agreement with his words for commitment to him and commitment to the truth he embodied and proclaimed. This is the difference between being a fan in the stands and a player on the field. It is easier to admire what Jesus said and did than to embrace the truth his teaching proclaims and live it.

Lest we be excessively hard on ourselves or others, it is well for us to remember the original twelve disciples did not always get it right. In story after story in the four Gospels, the disciples misunderstood. One of the twelve betrayed him, and when Jesus was arrested, ten fled the scene and one denied knowing him.

But when they stumbled, fell, and wandered off in the wrong direction, that was not the end of the story. Eleven of the twelve original disciples continued in their journey to live as servants of God. What made their recovery possible was that they did not deny their sin, and they were open to the grace of God transforming their living with more than forgiveness. They experienced what the New Testament describes as new life; their daily living was increasingly shaped by the grace of God made known in Jesus.

How can we be open to this grace-shaped new life happening in us? There are significant clues in the New Testament stories about the followers of Jesus coming together after the crucifixion and resurrection. Struggling to make sense of what had happened, they dug into the Hebrew Scriptures, trying to find some clues that would help them understand and enable them to move on with their lives. As they searched, they experienced being in the presence of the risen Christ or empowered by the Spirit of God.

So it has been across the centuries. People who earnestly yearn to make sense of life and are open to God's guidance as they read the Scriptures have received more than intellectual insight. Their living has been touched and shaped by the grace of God.

Since the writing of the Gospel of Matthew, the Sermon on the Mount has been especially helpful to people as, century after century, they have strived to discern God's will and become aware of God's grace. Through these teachings of Jesus, the life-transforming grace that changed the lives of the original disciples has impacted persons generation after generation. As individuals in each era have struggled to discern what these words of Jesus meant for their times and their lives, they have been encountered by the grace of God.

Because there is more grace available through these passages than can be grasped in one reading, Christians have not been content to read the Sermon on the Mount just once, but have returned to it again and again as long as they lived, more often than not discovering or rediscovering the truth of Christ and being encountered by grace time and again.

Our desires for meaning, for joy, for strength to endure, and for hope are among our deepest human longings. In the Sermon on the Mount, Jesus talks about what gives our living eternal meaning and enables our living to be blessed by enduring hope, strength, and joy. Whenever individuals discover that they are similarly blessed by their encounter with the grace of God through the Sermon on the Mount, there is astonishment not unike what the crowd in Matthew's Gospel experienced.

"And when Jesus finished these sayings, the crowds were astonished at his teaching, for he taught them as one who had authority, and not as their scribes" (Matt 7:28–29).

For Meditation and Conversation

1. What is it about this collection of sayings that astonished the crowd on that hillside long ago?

2. What astonishes you about these sayings?

3. As you look back on these forty chapters and your meditation and conversations about the wisdom of Jesus in Matthew 5–7, what gifts of grace have you received?

A Personal Postscript

MY JOURNEY WITH THE Sermon on the Mount began in seminary when I read the writings of Martin Luther and then spent an hour or two each week discussing what I had read with Dr. Van Harvey. One of the texts on which we spent hours was Luther's sermons dealing with Matthew 5–7.

My encounter with these sayings of Jesus moved to a deeper level when I became a pastor. In September 1963, at the ripe old age of twenty-seven, I was appointed by Bishop Paul Galloway to be the pastor of a congregation with 250 members, most of whom were thirty or more years older than I. With only a couple of years experience as an associate pastor, and just enough education to create in me the illusion that I knew a lot, I began my journey as a pastor among farmers and ranchers, businesspeople who served farmers and ranchers, and widows of farmers and ranchers. Few had college educations, but many of them had more knowledge of the Bible than I, and all of them had more experience with the struggles, troubles, and tragedies of life.

One of the major challenges I faced as a novice pastor was that I was going to have to prepare and preach each week not one sermon but two–– one on Sunday morning, and a different one on Sunday evening. I was just getting started so I had no file of sermons to draw on. Then I remembered that part of our Methodist heritage is the forty-four standard sermons that John Wesley published for the lay preachers of the Methodist movement in eighteenth-century England. Why not preach his sermons in my words? That would almost take care of the first year of evening sermons. So, week after week, I would outline one of the sermons, make copies of the outline (anyone remember the days of mimeograph machines?) to give to the members, and then try to preach it in my own words. Among the standard sermons were thirteen that Wesley wrote dealing with the Sermon on the Mount.

In 1964, as the season of Lent approached, I was aware that as pastor, I was expected to offer a Bible study. I had already learned that expecting the members of this congregation to do significant outside preparation was futile. What would be needed was the combination of a presentation that I would make and a conversation that the group would have. Why not explore the meaning in the beatitudes from the Sermon on the Mount? It was a classic passage that could easily fit into the limited time of Lent.

I looked at my fledgling personal library. What resources did I have that would be interesting to me and perhaps helpful to them? I had read Martin Luther's sermons dealing with the Sermon on the Mount while in seminary and John Wesley's in preparing for evening worship services. At a used bookstore, I had purchased volumes of sermons by Chrysostom, Augustine, and Calvin that contained what they had written about the beatitudes. On my shelves was *The Cost of Discipleship* by Dietrich Bonhoeffer, which contains his comments on Matthew 5–7 that I had been intending to read.

I was confident that the people who were likely to come to the study knew the beatitudes so well that they could almost recite them from memory. I knew I did not have the knowledge or the life experience that would offer much to their ongoing faith journey, but I could share what these Christian thinkers from across the centuries had written and use their insights as the basis for conversation.

Not long after the study was completed, I found myself draw-ing on what we had discussed when a slate of candidates sponsored by a Mexican-American group won both city council and school board elections, causing the tensions in that South Texas farming community to increase. Prejudices, fears, and old resentments created a climate of mistrust and hostility. As I moved about the community, I took on the unofficial role of mediator. In conversations with persons on both sides, I tried with my limited skill and knowledge to help people on either side of the divide understand the other.

It was not unusual for my efforts to be less than appreciated and often ineffective because of my lack of wisdom and skill or because of the depth of prejudice, fear, and resentment at work in individuals on both sides. That was the period in my life when I discovered that one definition of a mediator is he who has rocks thrown at him from both sides.

During that time, as I prayed about what our community was going through, I drew on what we had discussed during Lent, and I was encouraged by the wisdom and comforted by the grace conveyed in the beatitudes. It was the first time as an adult and as a pastor that I was aware of experiencing the Scriptures as a resource for the tough times I was going through.

Many years (and three assignments) later, in 1988, I became the senior pastor at Tarrytown United Methodist Church in Austin, Texas, where I discovered that I was expected to lead a Bible study between the two Sunday morning worship services. Once again, I turned to the beatitudes, but this time I went beyond them to examine the entire Sermon on the Mount through the eyes of Chrysostom, Augustine, Luther, Calvin, Wesley, and Bonhoeffer. Each week I would deal with a few verses.

While I was involved in the exploration of these sayings of Jesus, I was also dealing with fear and feelings of failure because my wife and I discovered our teenage son was addicted to drugs and alcohol. I am thankful to report that he has reclaimed his life and is now doing well. But for a few years it was rough for him, and for his mother and me.

Once again my involvement with the Sermon on the Mount was a source of wisdom and comfort. What I was going through led me to a deeper awareness of what it is to be poor in spirit, to mourn, and to hunger and thirst for a right relationship with God. I learned in a most personal way the wisdom of turning the other cheek and going the extra mile. Aware of my powerlessness in the midst of fear and anxiety, I grew in my understanding of Jesus' comments about the birds of the air and the wisdom of letting go and trusting God. In the midnight hours, when worry and fear robbed me of sleep, I discovered the healing of focusing on praying (not just saying) the Lord's Prayer, again and again, and when I could not do that, I would simply focus on this phrase from that prayer as I breathed in and out: "Thy will."

The Sermon on the Mount describes a way of living that is centered in trusting God so completely that one strives to do God's will. While from time to time I have abandoned this way of life and wandered off in some other directions, this passage, as much or more than others, continually calls me to reexamine my priorities.

To be human is to have to deal with temptations to be less and worse than God intends. The humanity of Jesus is perhaps most clearly seen in the stories of his being tempted (Matt 4:1–11 and 16:21–23). Certainly, being a pastor brings its own set of temptations. The ones that make the headlines have to do with scandals involving sex or money. But the more frequent temptations pastors have to deal with have to do with substituting being a successful leader of an organization for being faithful to God.

One of the questions that more than a few have asked me is, "What is it like to be the pastor of the governor?" Both the families of Governor George W. Bush and Governor Rick Perry worshipped in the church I served before I retired. Governor Bush's decision to run for the office of President brought more than a little attention to the congregation and to me.

When prominent public servants or leading business professionals are members of a congregation, there are at least two temptations that confront the pastor. One is to exploit them for the sake of gaining personal prestige and attracting their supporters to join. Another is to exploit them by using the pulpit to attack their policies and programs and thereby demonstrate to colleagues and other members the pastor's courage and social conscience credentials.

After much prayer, I became convinced that my responsibility as pastor to these persons who happened to be governors was no different than my responsibility as pastor to any other church member. As pastor, I am to do what I can to bring out the God-given best in each of them. When Governor Bush or Governor Perry participated in the congregation, they did so not as governor but as George Bush, child of God, or Rick Perry, child of God. And that is how I tried to deal with them.

"But," some have asked, "what about when you disagreed with the policies of their administrations?" In my role as pastor, I have found great wisdom in the Sermon of the Mount. Jesus said, "So whatever you wish that men would do to you, do so to them; for this is the law and the prophets."

Just as I do not want to be publicly attacked by those I view as friends and family, I do not use the pulpit bluntly to denounce church members, including a church member who happens to be the governor of the state. When I had serious concerns with a member regarding what he or she was doing or not doing, I did not attack from the pulpit. That seems to me a cowardly way because the person cannot talk back. Besides, it is an ineffective tactic because a public attack tends to entrench those with whom one disagrees rather than persuading them to change.

Therefore, I have tried to deal with members with whom I disagree in the way that I would want those who disagree with my positions to deal with me, including members who happen to be governors. This does not mean I avoid dealing with social concern issues, but it does mean that I try to deal with them in settings where those who disagree have the opportunity to talk back. I have found face-to-face conversation a more effective means of persuasion than public attacks. Besides, sometimes I am the one whose position needs to change once I learn all the facts.

The next chapter in my appreciation for the Sermon on the Mount has come since I retired. In June 2006, having turned seventy, I preached my last sermon as pastor of a congregation. Since then, I served three months as interim pastor of Coker United Methodist Church in San Antonio, and later I served eight months as pastor of the congregations in Yoakum and Hope. For four years, I was engaged by the Texas Methodist Foundation Institute for Clergy and Congregational Excellence to work with two groups of ten pastors. In all this work, I found myself drawing on wisdom from the Sermon on the Mount––wisdom about what blessing is and is not, about the way mourning done in faith is blessed with comfort, about forgiveness setting us free from the past and mercy enabling us to focus on positive possibilities.

I am confident that in whatever time I have remaining this side of death, I will continue to find wisdom and grace in the profound sayings of Jesus that we call the Sermon on the Mount.

Appendix

First Session (when the books are distributed)

1. Introductions:
   a. Name?
   b. What activities occupy most of your waking hours?
   c. Why are you participating in these readings and conversations?
2. Distribute books
3. Agree regarding the time and place to meet
4. Review the reading schedule
5. Agree regarding the group conversation agenda (see suggested agenda and modify it to fit the group)
6. Agree regarding the time to begin and end the group conversation
7. Agree to be present and participate in the conversation each week
8. Decide whether or not to have refreshments at each session, and if you have refreshments, who will bring them next session

For conversation at the first session:

- What attitudes and behaviors help one grow in grace and mature in faith?

- What attitudes and behaviors hinder one from growing in grace and maturing in faith?

- List prayer concerns on a whiteboard so that persons can make a list to take home for use in their daily prayers. As a group, pray (in silence, or someone speak a prayer) and conclude with the Lord's Prayer.

ONE EXAMPLE OF AN AGENDA FOR THE GROUP SESSIONS

Refreshments as people gather.

- List prayer concerns on a whiteboard so that persons can make a list to take home for use in their daily prayers. As a group, pray (in silence, or someone speak a prayer) and conclude with the Lord's Prayer.

- In unison, read the verses from Matthew that will be dealt with this session.

In small groups of three to five persons (preferably without spouses in the same small group), answer the following questions:

1. What questions or concerns do you have about the reading?

2. From your reflections at the end of each chapter this week, what insights did you have about yourself and your faith journey?

3. From this week's readings, identify what elicited a sense of hope and/or inner calm or peace within you.

4. Identify what in this week's readings strengthened or empowered you to face what you have to face.

5. What topics would this small group like the group as a whole to discuss?

In the total group:

1. List conversation topics from the small groups on a whiteboard.

2. Identify the topics to be discussed and in what order.

3. Converstaion by the total group.

    a. What did the author write that speaks to this topic?

    b. What insights and wisdom does the group have regarding this topic?

4. Remind one another of the material to be covered at the next group session.

5. Identify who brings refreshments next time.

Dismissal

One Possible Reading Schedule

Schedule the first session to distribute the books.

See the suggested agenda for the first session.

Set the reading schedule. Focus on one chapter per day each week. The following schedule, intended as an example, is tied to Lent:

> Wednesday before Lent, first group session (see first session agenda)
>
> Thursday through Wednesday, chapters 1–7
>
> Ash Wednesday, second group session
>
> Thursday through Wednesday, chapters 8–14
>
> Second Wednesday in Lent, third group session
>
> Thursday through Wednesday, chapters 15–21
>
> Third Wednesday in Lent, fourth group session
>
> Thursday through Wednesday, chapters 22–28
>
> Fourth Wednesday in Lent, fifth group session
>
> Thursday through Wednesday, chapters 29–35
>
> Fifth Wednesday in Lent, sixth group session
>
> Thursday through Wednesday, chapters 36–40
>
> Read "A Personal Postscript" on Monday of Holy Week
>
> Personal reflections about Matthew 5–7 on Tuesday
>
> Sixth Wednesday in Lent, seventh and final group session

One Possible Schedule for Conversations Dealing with
The Beatitudes

This suggested schedule focuses on one beatitude at each session. The group may want to combine beatitudes and have fewer sessions. See the suggested agenda for group sessions.

First Session:
> The books are distributed.
> See the suggested agenda for this session.

Reading for Second Session, Introduction:
> "Preparing for the Journey"
> "The Way Jesus Teaches" (5:1–2)

Reading for Third Session:
> "Blessed beyond Happiness" (5:2–3a)
> "The Importance of Need" (5:3)

Reading for Fourth Session:
> "Strength to Love" (5:4)

Reading for Fifth Session:
> "Disciplined Power" (5:5)

Reading for Sixth Session:
> "The Primary Hunger" (5:6)

Reading for Seventh Session:
> "Why Mercy Is Essential" (5:7)

Reading for Eighth Session:
> "The Way to Be Aware of God" (5:8)

Reading for Ninth Session:
> "The Obvious Children of God" (5:9)

Reading for Tenth Session:
> "Who Are Blessed?" (5:10–12)

Reading for Concluding Session *(optional)*:
> "Who Are the Salt of the Earth?" (5:13)
> "Being the Light of the World" (5:14–16)

One Possible Schedule for Conversations Dealing with
The Lord's Prayer

This suggested schedule focuses on one petition of the Lord's Prayer at each session. The group may want to combine petitions and have fewer sessions. See the suggested agenda for group sessions.

First Session:
The books are distributed
See the suggested agenda for this session.

Reading for Second Session, Introduction:
"Preparing for the Journey"
"The Way Jesus Teaches" (5:1–2)

Reading for Third Session:
"Prayer and Religious Pretensions" (6:5–8)

Reading for Fourth Session:
"Our Father" (6:9)

Reading for Fifth Session:
"Thy Kingdom Come; Thy Will Be Done" (6:10)

Reading for Sixth Session:
"Give Us This Day Our Daily Bread" (6:11)

Reading for Seventh Session:
"Forive Us . . . As We Have Forgiven" (6:12)

Reading for Eighth Session:
"Lead Us Not into Temptation but Deliver Us from Evil " (6:13a)

Reading for Ninth Session:
"For Thine Is the Power and the Glory Forever. Amen." (6:13b)

Reading for Concluding Session *(optional)*:
"The Forgiven Are to Forgive" (6:14–15)
"Phony Faithfulness" (6:16–18)

Bibliography

Aikman, David. *Great Souls: Six Who Changed the Century.* Nashville, TN: Word,1998.

Allen, Joseph L. *War: A Primer for Christians.* Dallas: Southern Methdodist University Press, 2001.

Augustine. *Confessions.* Translated by Henry Chadwick. Oxford: Oxford University Press, 1998.

———. *A Select Library of the Nicene and Post-Nicene Fathers of the Christian Church.* Vol. 6, *Saint Augustin: Sermon on the Mount. Harmony of the Gospels. Homilies on the Gospels.* Edited by Philip Schaff. New York: Christian Literature Co., 1886.

Bonhoeffer, Dietrich. *The Cost of Discipleship.* Rev. ed. Translated by R. H. Fuller. New York: Macmillan, 1963.

———. *The Cost of Discipleship.* Translated by R. H. Fuller and Irmgard Booth. New York: Macmillan, 1963.

———. *Life Together.* Translated by John W. Doberstein. London: SCM Press, 1956.

Calvin, John. *A Harmony of the Synoptic Gospels.* Calvin's Commentaries. Lafayette, IN: Calvin Publications, n.d.

Chrysostom, John. *The Preaching of Chrysostom: Homilies on the Sermon on the Mount.* Edited by Jaroslav Pelikan. Philadelphia: Fortress, 1967.

Eberhard, Bethge. *Dietrich Bonhoeffer: Man of Vision, Man of Courage.* New York: Harper & Row, 1970.

Frankl, Viktor E. *Man's Search for Meaning: An Introduction to Logotherapy.* New York: Washington Square Press, 1964.

Kierkegaard, Søren. *Purity of Heart.* Translated by Douglas V. Steere. New York: Harper Torchbooks, 1964.

Luther, Martin. *Luther's Works.* Vol. 21, *The Sermon on the Mount and the Magnificat.* Translated and edited by Jaroslav Pelikan. St. Louis: Concordia, 1956.

Wesley, John. *Explanatory Notes upon the New Testament.* London: Epworth, 1958.

———. *Forty-Four Sermons: Sermons on Several Occasions.* London: Epworth, 1958.

———. *The Works of John Wesley, Vol. 1, Sermons 1–33.* Edited by Albert C. Outler. Nashville: Abingdon, 1984.

2011 public letter by George H. Freeman, General Secretary of the World Methodist Council. http://worldmethodistcouncil.org.